A Student`s Guide for Assignments, Projects and Research in Business and Management

5th Edition

by

Arthur Adamson

MBE PhD MSc BA DMS FIMgt CIPD TCert

Arthur Adamson

1995

First published by Thamesman Publications

1st Edition   1977
2nd Edition   1980
3rd Edition   1986
4th Edition   1990

1st Impression   1990
2nd Impression 1991
3rd Impression 1992

Published by Arthur Adamson

4th Impression 1994

5th Edition 1995

ISBN 1 871053 05 6

Printed in Great Britain by

Allinson & Wilcox
Queen Street Louth Lincs LN11 9BN

Published by

Arthur Adamson
5 Windsor Mews Church Street Louth Lincs LN11 9AY
Tel: 01507 600385 Fax: 01507 606518

CONTENTS

PURPOSES

I assume that as part of a programme of education or training in business or management you are required to conduct an individual activity and at the end submit some written product. The activity may be called an 'assignment', 'project' or 'research' and the product may be called a 'paper', 'report', 'dissertation' or 'thesis'. The terms used vary among academic institutions and professional bodies, sometimes representing ascending academic or professional levels in the length of time allocated to the activity and the size of the written outcome. There are some differences among the various disciplines and written outcomes, for example in finance, marketing, production and human resources. However they all share a common purpose and it is possible to identify many common practical methods, pitfalls, experiences and conventions. This guidebook aims to give you a framework within which you can approach such an activity and compose the written outcome. Beyond that framework you may of course need to consult specialist tutors or textbooks appropriate to the nature of the studies and the level of the activity. A bibliography of suggested texts is given at the end of Part 4.

For simplicity I will refer to the activity as the 'project' and to the written outcome as the 'report'.

It is important at this stage that you understand why academic and professional bodies now increasingly use this type of activity in their learning and assessment systems, especially where the aim of the programme is to prepare the student for an occupation or job. In the learning process the project is seen as an effective means to bring together the knowledge and skills you are acquiring in your studies and to give you the opportunity to apply them to the real world. This 'transfer of learning' is vital if the programme is aimed to prepare you for a job as an 'expert'. For assessment the way in which you conduct the project and present it in the written report will probably be a significant part of the pass/fail decision - whether or not you achieve the qualification offered by the programme. I hope from this that you will see that the project and the report are quite distinct. The project is a personal activity, usually over a period of time, in which you are developing an expertise that will be valuable to you in a job. The report is a document that you produce at the end of the project to persuade your assessors that you are developing that expertise at the required level and merit the qualification offered.

In the following pages I deal with the processes common to projects, the way in which you could select and conduct your project, and the composition and checking of your report. I then set out the conventions of academic reports and finally give an example of a report. For convenience I have illustrated the project and report in the field of human resources and finance, about which most people have some knowledge and where the outcome of sound investigation and persuasive reporting have obvious benefits. However, the principles apply in all fields of study.

There are additional long-term benefits for you if you are entering an occupation or job. You will frequently meet real issues and problems in your employment. If you can deal with them with a systematic investigation and then present a persuasive report to your peers and superiors, your reputation as an expert will be established and your career will be more likely to advance.

THE SUPERVISOR

Normally a member of the tutorial staff will be appointed to supervise you during your project. Your supervisor is an important resource who will be able to give you detailed advice on how to arrange and conduct the project and produce the report. As an expert in the specific field of study he or she will be able to give you advice beyond the bounds of this guide. He cannot do the work for you, but as the project progresses the supervisor can help considerably as a sounding board against which you can try out your ideas and plans. He can also suggest sources of information that you may not be aware of, or indicate lines of thought that you may not have considered, or ask questions that will force you to crystalize and justify your ideas and direction.

You should consult your supervisor at regular intervals throughout, but as supervisors are notoriously busy and elusive persons, you should make appointments for specific dates and times. A project can be a lonely and sometimes frustrating activity with periods of inertia and delays that have to be countered. Set-backs and competing priorities can easily deflect you from getting on with the work. Appointments with your supervisor act as deadlines to motivate you to achieve particular stages of the project. They also commit your supervisor to giving you due attention and make it clear to him that you are approaching the task seriously. The importance of regular consultation cannot be over-emphasised and it is especially important that you discuss the draft of your report with your supervisor before you submit the final version.

If you are an exceptionally gifted or lucky student you may ignore your supervisor, but experience shows that students who do so tend to be less successful in their projects through going off track, over-running the allocated time or producing an inadequate report. You should also bear in mind that your supervisor has some influence on the assessment of your project: he may be the person who assesses your report at the end. Even if there is a separate external assessor, your supervisor will be consulted and can often give helpful comments on the effort you put into the project or on unexpected snags and obstacles you met. You would be wise to make your supervisor your ally by involving him in every stage of the project and report.

FRUSTRATION

Like every other student who embarks on a project you will have set-backs, periods of anxiety and frustration, and intervals of inertia, both in conducting the project and in writing up the report. It is rarely fatal. Talk to your fellow-students and you will have the benefit of finding that they have the same worries and problems. If it gets too bad talk to your supervisor. If all else fails re-read the appropriate section of this book and force yourself to hit the next deadline.

ELATION

The acceptance of a completed report on a successful project will be a highlight of your programme. It will compensate you for all the sweat and tears. It will be your own creation - it might even make you famous. Go for it.

OUTLINE

A project is not unique to educational and training programmes: its purpose is the development of an expertise to be used in real life. It is conducted through an investigatory process that is commonly used by all kinds of experts: professional specialists, managers, researchers, technologists, doctors, detectives. The process is the key to their effectiveness and if you can grasp this basic process you have a model for carrying out your project. Within its framework you can develop your own specialist objectives and research techniques for your investigations. You will also learn how to apply the process to the problems and opportunities you will meet in your later work as a specialist. Ability to identify a problem or opportunity, to investigate it thoroughly, and to present a persuasive report about it often marks out the individual as a valuable asset to an organization. Many successful senior executives have gained their promotions by displaying this ability.

An investigator begins by defining clearly the problem or the opportunity (the Issue) and the aim of the investigation (the resolution of the problem or the exploration of the opportunity). He or she then summons up all the relevant expert knowledge he has available (Concepts), while at the same time observing and analysing the facts and data about the situation (Evidence). By bringing the concepts to bear on the evidence, and vice versa, (Evaluation) he is able to form his expert opinion about the issue (Conclusions) from which he can recommend actions to be taken to deal with the issue (Recommendations). He will then have to communicate his investigation and results to those concerned with the issue (Report). Figure 1 illustrates the process as a simple model.

ISSUE

I use the word 'issue' to indicate an important matter, the resolution of which is desired by a number of people or an individual. As examples:

A nation may be concerned about high inflation, a company may be undecided about putting a new invention into production, a local community may be upset about some local pollution, a family may be faced with the decision of whether or not to move to a larger house, an individual may see an opportunity to move to a better job. Each of these issues is important to the particular people concerned and they seek to have the issue dealt with.

In an organization issues arise usually through changes in its external environment or in its internal structure. Such changes may pose threats (problems)

about the organization's well-being or effectiveness: conversely they may open up opportunities to gain advantage for the organization and its members. The problem becomes an issue to be resolved, preferably by expert investigation rather than by snap decision. The opportunity becomes an issue to be investigated in terms of possible costs and benefits before a decision is taken. With the problem the issue may sometimes be stated like 'Such-and-such is a threat. What can we do to prevent or avoid it?' An opportunity can best be expressed as a hypothesis, ie, an untested theory, like 'If we do so-and-so, we should gain such-and-such.'

---

1. ISSUE
Problem or Opportunity (Hypothesis)
and Statement of Aim

2. CONCEPTS
Expert Knowledge
& Theory
`The literature`

3. EVIDENCE
Observation, description
& analysis of situation
`The facts`

4. EVALUATION
of Evidence against Concepts - 'The implications'

5. CONCLUSIONS
Opinion of situation about Issue from Evaluation -

'Possible treatment'

6. RECOMMENDATIONS
Actions that should be taken - 'Chosen treatment'

7. REPORT
Written and/or Oral

Figure 1. The Investigatory Process

For example:

A company may be troubled by excessive absenteeism and bad time-keeping among its employees. The management may see this as a serious problem: 'We must do something about high absenteeism because it is increasing production costs and causing delays.' and set about resolving it by investigating its causes and effects and considering possible solutions. In the same field, a company may note that many of its local competitors have introduced flexible working hours for their employees. The management may see this practice as a possible opportunity for benefits and express it as a hypothesis: 'If we introduced flexible working hours we would have a happier workforce and we would reduce absenteeism, lateness and labour costs.' It would then investigate the various techniques, the costs and benefits to the company and employees and then decide whether or not it would be worthwhile to introduce the system.

As another example:

The headteacher of a school might become conscious of relatively low attainment by the pupils in relation to other schools. The issue would be a problem to be resolved: 'Our attainment rate is too low in relation to other schools.' Conversely the headteacher may return from an educational conference with the idea that computer-based learning has great possibilities and might ask a member of staff to investigate its possible introduction into the school: 'If we introduced computer-based learning it would help pupils to learn more easily.'

As the issue is the starting point of the investigatory process, you will see that the precision with which you define it is important, as all the rest flows from it. With a problem you have to keep asking yourself 'Is this really the problem?' With an opportunity you need to define and refine the hypothesis so that you have a clear focus for you investigation. As you work through the investigation you may discover that you have not focused on the real problem or that your hypothesis has missed out an important factor: you may then have to redefine the issue.

CONCEPTS

We build 'concepts' in our minds. They are drawn from our knowledge, experience, beliefs and perceptions of the world around us. The wider our knowledge and experience, the more and better concepts we are able to construct. Because concepts are subject to our own perceptions, they are sometimes difficult to frame in words - for example I consider that I need to define to you what I mean by the concepts 'issue' and 'concept'. We obtain our concepts from what we hear, read, see and experience. To some extent they are our own ideas, but most of them we take from other people, where we consider them to be acceptable, but even then we may modify them to fit them in with our own ideas. The array of concepts available to us in a particular area of knowledge can be immense: within our own memories, from books, tapes, films, publications (the 'literature'), computer data banks or from enquiring of other people with experience or expertise in the area.

For example:

If you are are considering the layout of your garden you may rely simply on your past experience: on the other hand you may watch television programmes about gardening, or consult books on gardening, or talk to you neighbours about their garden successes and failures, or even consult a gardening expert. The wider you search for knowledge about garden layout, the better should be your concepts of an ideal garden layout, although in the end your concepts will be decided by your acceptance, modification or rejection of what you have seen and heard.

Those concepts of a garden layout are mainly about physical matters, but we also have many concepts about processes such as attitude surveys, grievance procedures, recruitment and selection, or phenomena such as labour turnover, absenteeism, company growth, or policies about finance, production and marketing, or relationships such as management, leadership, employee relations. We also have more abstract concepts such as love, motivation, power, influence. You will appreciate that you have your own understanding and use of each of these concepts, affected by your experience, values and perception. Equally, other people may understand them differently because of their personal experiences, beliefs and perceptions. In using a concept you need first to define carefully to yourself just what it means and what its value and limitations are and, secondly, to explain to any others concerned your interpretation, use and limits. They may not agree with you completely, but at least they will be able to understand your viewpoint.

We frequently use the word 'model' in relation to concepts, as we seek to find ideals. We use models to crystalize our concepts about a particular area of knowledge and understanding. In this sense a model is an abstraction from reality of significant parts and factors, and their relationships. This enables us to justify, explain and reconstruct the reality, but a model is a simplification and is rarely completely true. We constantly try out our conceptual models against our experience and learning and so modify, refine and improve them. They then become more and more useful to us in explaining and recreating reality. As concepts are 'in the mind' we need often to express them in words, or represent them in drawings, or programme them into a computer, or build them into a physical model. For example:

As you successively live in or visit different houses you may begin to form your concept of the ideal house you would eventually like to own, ie, you have a model in your mind. At any time you could explain this model in words, or you could draw a diagram of it in various scales of detail, or you might build a model of it in wood. As time goes on you would modify and improve your conceptual model and so your explanation or reconstruction of it would be modified and improved. If the time came when you could afford to have it built, you could explain your ideal in words and diagrams to an architect and a builder, in considerable detail. They in turn would of course try to advise you to modify your model from their concepts of what is practicable within the available resources and building regulations.

In the case of the other non-physical types of concepts given above, you will see that you could build a model of the relationships of management, leadership, power and influence. Another model might cover business policy and finance. Another might incoporate attitude surveys, absenteeism and labour turnover: another could connect employee relations, grievance procedures and motivation. For each you would begin by constructing it in your thoughts: you would then have to translate it into words or visual images to explain it.

One main purpose of undergoing programmes of education or training is to improve the array of concepts we have available. As we 'practise' our profession or 'gain experience' we are also extending and refining the array of conceptual models we can call on, not just in our memories but also in our knowledge of the sources we can turn to if we wish to review the best and most up-to-date concepts in a particular area of knowledge. One of the intrinsic rewards of being an 'expert' is the satisfaction of constantly improving and adding to one's tool-kit of conceptual models.

There are of course those people who dismiss 'concepts', 'theories' and 'academic points of view', and say that only the facts matter. This ignores the point that concepts are created from experience of facts and that they give rise to theories that seek to explain relationships among facts. The role of the academic is to gather together research and the experience of practitioners in a particular field of knowledge in order to create conceptual models that can feed back to practitioners to help in explaining and predicting reality. The practitioner can call on such available conceptual models to add to his or her own to help illuminate, explain and resolve a real issue. Those who ignore the value and availability of external concepts tend to re-invent the wheel, or at worst fail to see that better types of wheel bearings and tyres have been found.

Facts on their own are of little value until they are harnessed to concepts. For example:

Portraits of Oliver Cromwell show that he had a wart on his nose: this is fact but useless information until it is linked with the concepts from various bodies of knowledge. The medical expert might produce theories about the state of cosmetic surgery in Cromwell's days; the psychologist might consider concepts *about the effects of physical appearance on personality, or why Cromwell did not insist on it being left out of his portrait; the art historian might propose a fashion of portrait painting at that time that insisted on representation being realistic, warts and all.*

In the investigatory process the investigator will summon up the concepts that appear relevant to the issue. These in turn will give him or her indications of the evidence he needs to seek and as the facts emerge he may reject some concepts as irrelevant or he may extend his search for more concepts to explain and guide the investigation. The more expert he is, the more relevant concepts he can call up and deploy. However it will be seen that this action takes place in parallel with and linked to the search for evidence (the facts).

EVIDENCE

Evidence is the 'facts' relating to the issue to be resolved. While concepts are generalities that might illuminate the particular issue, the evidence is about the real situation surrounding that issue. The quality of the investigation will depend much on the stringency with which the evidence is sought out and sifted. In legal terms it must be 'best evidence': hearsay and circumstantial evidence may be dangerous grounds on which to make judgements. The evidence must be of the same quality and scope as the concepts, and must have equal priority. Just as there are those who mistakenly dismiss concepts in favour of facts, equally there are those who rely too much on theory in coming to conclusions: 'Don't trouble me with the facts.'

The collection of evidence involves observation and description. To be useful it then has to be analysed and arranged to identify relationships: it also has to be stored in such a way that it can be recalled and reviewed in various combinations. Clearly it should not be collected randomly and haphazardly: where possible a method or system should be devised, perhaps tried out first by a sample or 'pilot' survey, so that the right evidence is collected, in the best sequence, without overlooking important facts.

The knowledge and experience that helps build our concepts are filtered and modified by our perceptions. Our perceptions may also affect our observation, description, arrangement and analysis of the facts that emerge about an issue as we assemble the evidence. It is too easy to generalise from a limited number of facts, or to accept dubious information because it fits in with our concepts, or reject some facts that are uncomfortable, or to see relationships between facts, or to confuse correlation with causality, or to accept other people's descriptions when we could look ourselves. The expert tries to be as objective as possible in getting at the real evidence, by using the best possible means of observing and measuring, carefully checked, and by using a system designed for the collection of evidence.

Particular specialisms develop their own methods (or 'methodology') to search for relevant evidence. Doctors are trained to examine patients in a systematic way according to the general nature of the complaint; scientists have developed various techniques for their research; social scientists commonly use carefully devised questionnaire techniques; engineers and technologists use standardised tests; the police have a standard procedure for examining the scene of a crime. Many specialists now use computers to store and analyse their evidence, and many call on computerised data banks to examine evidence from parallel situations.

In parallel and in concert with the summoning up of concepts, the investigator uses a systematic method to collect and analyse all the evidence relevant to the issue. As he or she proceeds his concepts will indicate what evidence he needs: as the evidence emerges it will indicate to him which concepts are relevant and what others need to be deployed.

EVALUATION

The evaluation stage is the weighing up of the evidence in the light of the concepts, and vice versa, to assess the 'value' of each. The evidence is valued against the yardstick of the concept: the concept is valued against the yardstick of the evidence. In this interplay, the practitioner expert will have a different aim from the academic researcher. The practitioner is using the best concepts to draw out the right implications from the evidence: the academic is using the best evidence from as many sources as possible to test out and so reject, refine or reinforce a concept. The student doing a project for a real company problem or opportunity may have both aims: to improve his or her array of concepts and to identify for the company the implications of a set of evidence.

Evaluation requires self-discipline to restrict the drawing of implications to the limits of the concept and the limits of the evidence. Going beyond this is 'jumping to conclusions' and unfortunately is a common mistake. For example:

As a train watcher you may time a high speed train passing a fixed point as taking 3 seconds (evidence). You may have available the knowledge that the standard length of such a train is 450 feet and that 88 feet per second is 60 miles per hour (concepts). You could therefore draw the implication that the train was travelling at about 100 miles per hour (evaluation). You would not be entitled to deduce from this limited evidence and the limits of the two concepts deployed where the train would be stopping next or the colour of the engine driver's socks. You would need other

sets of concepts and evidence to deduce these.

The investigator might use a number of combinations of concepts and evidence. Each set of concepts and their related evidence would produce implications limited to that set. He or she would then have to inter-relate all the implications to see what overall picture they produced.

CONCLUSIONS

Conclusions are the expression of opinion about the issue, based on the evaluation of the concepts and evidence so far. There may be several sets of concepts+evidence=implications. The implications may be disjointed and so more concepts may have to be brought into play to establish their relationships and the overall implications. If the picture is not complete it may be necessary to search for further concepts and evidence before coming to conclusions about the issue. Once the overall picture is complete it can be set out in three logical steps.

The first step in the Conclusions is to express an informed opinion about what the overall situation is in relation to the issue. Again it must be stringently limited to the implications drawn from concepts and evidence sets and to any new concepts applied to them overall. No new evidence can be introduced in this stage.

The second step is to express opinion about what could happen if the present overall situation were to continue. Again other concepts may have to be deployed but again it must be a logical step from opinion about the overall situation and no new evidence can be introduced.

The third step is to consider what possible courses of action could be taken to resolve the problem or opportunity, including where possible for each the resultant costs and benefits, or advantages and disadvantages, or likely effects. Again concepts might enable a wide range of options to be explored to estimate their possible costs and benefits, their pros and cons, and their constraints.

There is obviously a discipline about conclusions: they must be related to the issue and they must be founded on the concepts deployed and the evidence examined. The investigator takes three steps in the conclusion stage by forming opinion on:

1. What the overall situation really is.

2. What could happen as a result.

3. What could be done about it
   (exploration of possible courses of action).

It is significant that at this stage, in steps 2 and 3, the key word is 'could'. The word 'should' is reserved for the Recommendations that follow.

RECOMMENDATIONS

An investigation could end at the Conclusions stage, leaving it to others to decide what should be done to resolve the issue on the basis of the Conclusion's opinions about the overall situation, what could happen and what could be done. However investigators are usually required to make recommendations, ie to put their expertise 'on the line' and say decisively what should be done (as distinct from what could be done) to resolve the issue.

The Recommendations therefore follow logically from the Conclusions and no new discussion, concepts or evidence can be introduced at this stage. It will be clear that this is possible only if conclusions have been properly formed. Any recommendations must be limited to choices from the possible courses of action that have been explored in the final step of the Conclusions stage.

EXAMPLE OF AN INVESTIGATION

As an example of the investigation of an issue:

A patient who has a medical problem that worries him or her will visit a doctor. The issue is important to the patient and he presents it to the doctor as a problem which he hopes the doctor can resolve as the appropriate expert.

Immediately the doctor will begin to call up medical concepts from his or her training, knowledge and practice that might explain the patient's condition. Simultaneously he begins a systematic search for evidence about the condition: asking for more details about the symptoms and the circumstances in which they occur, consulting the patient's notes about the medical history and general health, and examining the patient physically in a systematic way. Each bit of evidence will be evaluated against relevant concepts to find the implications for the patient's state of health. Some evidence may be discarded as irrelevant: some concepts may be eliminated as inappropriate. Until the implications make up a satisfactory picture of the patient's state the parallel search for evidence and concepts would continue: for further concepts the doctor may consult his medical library, colleagues or specialists; for further evidence X-rays and analysis of blood and urine may be employed. When the doctor is satisfied that all the implications fit together he may then call on overall conceptual models to form an opinion about the ailment - his conclusions.

In expressing his conclusions to the patient the doctor would first tell him what specific ailment he is suffering - the diagnosis - what the situation is.

He would then explain the likely progress of the ailment if it continues as it is - the prognosis - what could happen as a result.

Then he would discuss with the patient several possible courses of action to alleviate the ailment: by rest or by medication or by reference to various specialists or by hospital treatment. For each he would explain the likely costs and outcomes, the risks and advantages, the immediacies and the waiting times - the possible treatments and their possible results - what could be done about it, with likely outcomes.

Finally from the possible courses of action he would recommend that the patient follow a particular course of treatment that is satisfactory and most beneficial to the patient - recommended treatment - what should be done about it.

The patient would not be satisfied if the doctor simply listened to his initial description of his problem and then said 'Here is a prescription, take the tablets twice a day and come back to see me next week if it is not better'. The patient needs to be persuaded that the doctor has made a thorough investigation and can justify the prescribed treatment. The patient therefore expects the doctor to explain the investigation, conclusions and recommendations if he is to trust his expertise and follow the treatment. The investigation has to be reported, fully, to the patient whose issue it is.

REPORT

The aim of an investigation is to examine a particular issue and to decide how it should be resolved. When satisfactory Conclusions have been reached and where appropriate sound Recommendations have been made, the aim of the investigation will have been achieved. There is now a new aim - the aim of the Report. This aim is to persuade others that the issue was correctly identified, that an expert investigation has been carried through, that convincing and comprehensive conclusions have been reached, and that recommended actions should be implemented.It is not enough for the investigator to say 'This is the issue and these are my recommendations.' Even as an expert he or she must convince those who are to stand the cost, effort and consequences that they should accept his advice. He needs therefore to construct a persuasive report, usually written but sometimes oral or both.

INVESTIGATION	REPORT	
Stages	Essential Elements	Optional Extras
1.ISSUE	TITLE	ACKNOWLEDGEMENTS ABSTRACT or SUMMARY CONTENTS
	INTRODUCTION	
2.CONCEPTS 3.EVIDENCE 4.EVALUATION	MAIN SECTIONS	METHOD
5.CONCLUSIONS	CONCLUSIONS	
6.RECOMMENDATIONS	RECOMMENDATIONS	
		APPENDICES

Figure 2. Relationship between the Investigation and its Report

The report has to carry the reader through the investigation in such a way that he or she is convinced of its thoroughness and expertise. It must be introduced with enough background information to enable the reader to understand the circumstances, a clear definition of the issue problem or opportunity, and a statement of what the investigation aims to achieve. The main part of the report will then carry the reader through all the concepts deployed, the evidence found and examined, and the implications arising from their evaluation. Finally it will draw these all together in the conclusions and then make its recommendations, which must relate to the issue posed in the introduction.

In providing a report to other experts in the same field or in the same company, the report may limit explanations about background and concepts that the potential readers may already be familiar with. However in most circumstances the investigator will need to set the scene, explain and justify all the concepts used and give all the necessary detailed evidence, on the assumption that the reader is a sceptical lay person who has to be convinced of the stringency and expert level of the investigation. This is also the case with the report of a student project, where an assessor has to be convinced that the student has developed the required level of knowledge, understanding and skill.

There are conventions about the structure, content and style of reports on investigations. Those most widely used in organizations are similar to those required for academic purposes; the latter are a little more specific in their requirements and are set out in Part 5 of this guide.

In the report of an investigation, certain elements of the structure are essential; additionally there are optional extras that can be placed in the structure if the investigation and the report are more comprehensive. The essential elements are the title, introduction, main sections, conclusions and, sometimes, recommendations. Optional extras are acknowledgements, contents, summary, method, references and appendices. Figure 2 shows the relationship between the investigatory process and the report.

ARRANGING A PROJECT

Choice of Topic Area

In the case of some short assignments, the topic area and even the issue may be specified by the tutorial staff, leaving you little room for manoeuvre in the choice of topic. However in most projects you will be expected to decide the topic and arrange the project yourself, with the agreement of the tutorial staff and your supervisor.

Two main considerations arise in trying to decide on a project topic: what facilities you will have, in time and access to organizations, to carry out an investigation, and what area of subject theory interests you most. It is necessary to have facilities to carry out the 'field work'. If your investigation is to be a 'library study' in which you do not require access to an organization or organizations, you will have greater freedom. But it is usual to expect projects to be carried out in the reality of an organization. In those circumstances you will need an organization that will allow you to intervene in its activities and have access to its staff and information. The more an organization sees your project as offering useful findings for its own purposes, the more likely it will be to welcome and assist you. It is easier and more enjoyable to embark on a project within an area of knowledge that you find interesting and relevant to your future. Arriving at a topic that will satisfy both you and an organization may take some time, and a number of alternatives should be considered and discussed with your supervisor, before settling for any one.

Ideas

Discussion with your tutors and fellow-students may help you to arrive at possible topics but you may feel apprehensive about your ability to work in isolation on a project. Your college or university library probably will hold copies of past students` reports on their projects, dissertations or theses. These are invaluable sources to stimulate ideas for your project. Select from the lists those at your level and subject area. Look through them for ideas about issues and methods. As successful reports they should give you a clearer view about standards, scope and length of a project. This should reassure you about your ability to achieve equally successful work.

Project Proposals

When you have ideas about possible topics and potential host organizations you should write down each as a project proposal, covering the following suggested points:

- Issue - a problem or opportunity ,with some background information.

- Aim - what is to be achieved, the scope and limitations.

- Value to the host organization.

- Value to yourself.

- Concept areas available - course work, literature, good practice.

- Evidence to be sought - data and analysis.

- Methods - methodology, timetable.

- Resources needed - from host and yourself.

You should boil each proposal down to one side of a sheet of A4 paper so that you can discuss each with your supervisor and the particular host organization. Once you have made your choice you can then build on the proposal with greater detail. If it crashes you will have the others available to fall back on.

Timetable

You must consider the element of time. First, it usually takes some time, even weeks or months, to settle the matter of the topic area and host organization and reach agreement with your supervisor. This is even before you begin the project, so you cannot start too early on the search. Secondly, you must consider how much time you will have, full-time and/or part-time, to complete the investigation and write up the report. It always takes longer than you estimate, because you meet unexpected obstacles and setbacks, and you may be too ambitious in the scope of your investigation. Many students also underestimate the time it takes to draft, write and produce copies of the report. You will probably be required to submit the final report by a deadline: it is important therefore that you decide on a project that you will be able to investigate and write up within the time available, and again you cannot start too early.

At this point you should draw up an outline timetable for the stages of your project, starting backwards from the date by which your final report has to be submitted for assessment. Figure 4 suggests the proportion of time you should allow for each stage. You may be surprised to see that the 'fieldwork' is a relatively small amount in the middle of the project. This underlines the time consuming work of the preparatory stages and the evaluation and report production stages.

AGREEMENT OF ISSUE WITH HOST ORGANIZATION

If you are being allowed to carry out a project in an organization you must remember constantly that you are an outsider who is costing the organization time and effort to help you. Remember that you are not necessarily seen as an expert consultant who has come to save the organization and solve its problems: you are getting something from the organization and its members for your benefit. Tread carefully at first until you become familiar with the climate. When you visit the organization or its departments be well prepared in advance about what you want to ask or be shown. The more efficient and business-like you appear, the more you will be accepted. The more courteous and understanding you are with individuals, the more co-operation you will receive. You should consider how you dress and speak, and always be careful about making appointments and keeping to time. When you are about to make your first visit to the organization, do some homework about it: what are its history, purposes and activities; what are its general structure, size and locations; what are its relationships with the economy and society generally; who are the senior managers; what information is available about the people you will first meet? This will demonstrate your efficiency and much of the information will be useful later. The organization and its members will judge you by their standards: the sooner you can come to terms with those standards, the sooner they will accept and co-operate with you and the faster will be your progress.

Having generated ideas for a possible topic area and possible issues, the approval of the organization is essential. The management must see it as important with some benefits to them to offset the intervention and administrative costs that will be incurred by your activities. Constraints on management's freedom of action are numerous: relations with external organizations and customers or clients; the attitudes of their superiors; security of information; the motivation of employees; the state of industrial relations. Management may not wish to proceed with a particular issue in the face of difficult constraints. They may ask you to take on some specific issue and you will need to discuss this in terms of your own requirements before you agree.

One difficulty you may encounter is agreement on an issue that meets the requirements of your education or training programme and its qualification. This underlines the need to engage your supervisor in the initial arrangements. If the organization requests the investigation of a problem there is no difficulty beyond agreeing the scope within the time available: the issue is a problem; the aim of the investigation is to enquire into its magnitude and extent, and to find a solution.

Similarly, if the organization says they are considering a particular course of action, the issue is an opportunity hypothesis 'If this action were to be taken, these benefits would result'; the aim of the investigation is to find out if it is true or not, and if true to recommend how it could be implemented. Another type of proposal by the organization could be the review of some process, procedure or system previously installed. This issue could also be framed as a hypothesis: 'The such process is operating effectively'; the aim of the investigation is then to find out if this is true or not and to recommend possible improvements. Another type is a request to design a process, procedure or system. Again the issue can be framed as a hypothesis: 'if the such process were designed and installed, it would give such benefits'; the aim of the investigation is then to find out if this is true and to recommend a particular design in detail.

When an issue has been agreed, you should then seek detailed agreements to avoid misunderstanding and possible hindrance to your project. Details should include your access to information; what information is confidential and how it may be included or not in your report; who will be your contact person within the organization; how people in the organization will be notified of your clearance to carry out the project; what facilities you may have for assembling data, typing and reproduction, printing, travel and expenses; the broad timetable; and the organization's requirements to see a draft of your report and receive copies of the final version. While you should try to persuade the organization to give you firm commitments you should also seek to keep for yourself some freedom of movement to modify the issue or its scope if you find snags as you proceed. If you are embarking on a major project you should involve your supervisor in the making of the agreements and, if possible, have the agreements recorded in writing.

Two items that should always be clearly agreed and recorded are:

The Issue - what is the problem or opportunity (hypothesis)?

The Aim of the Investigation - What do you hope to achieve about the Issue?

You would be wise to write these down prominently in some place where you see them constantly, for example on the front of your notebook or on a card on your desk. This will help to keep you on the rails. You should review them frequently to see if either could be more precisely worded. If a major change proves necessary you should discuss it with your supervisor and the host organization.

13

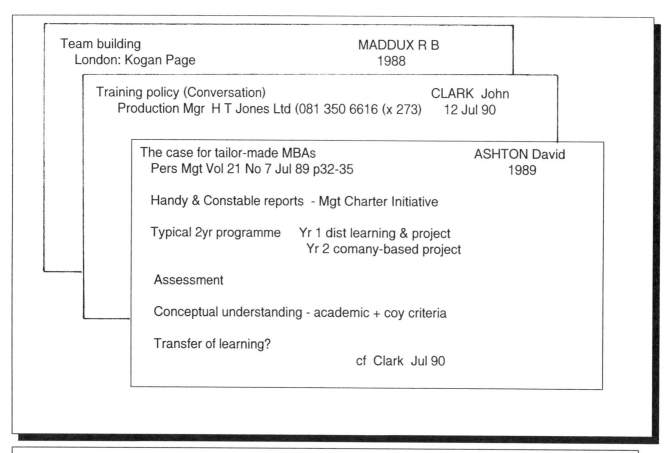

Figure 3. Project Data Record Card System   (8in x 5in (or A5) cards or A4 or A5 loose-leaf sheets)

PREPARATORY STUDY

Recording

Before embarking on the investigation it is important that you decide on a method for recording the concepts and evidence you gather so that you can retrieve, categorise and use them at later stages. I recommend that you use a reporter type notebook, that you carry around with you, for jotting down ideas and information as you come across them, for making notes when you are interviewing or consulting people, and for aide-memoirs on what you will be looking for on your next visit to libraries, places or people. Your problem will not be to obtain enough information, but how to sift, classify and retrieve it. I recommend for this that you use a system of loose-leaf sheets or cards on which to record your information from your notebook or direct from other sources. The Author-Date system outlined in the Conventions in Part 5 is particularly appropriate for this. For source material you should record exactly: author's name, date of publication, title of document, place and name of publisher, and sometimes page numbers. For opinions expressed by people consulted, the name, job title and organization, date of interview, place and telephone number should be recorded. You should discipline yourself to record systematically right from the beginning: it is very frustrating and time-consuming to remember later in the project that you read or heard something that is highly relevant and

then find that you cannot trace it. The use of the author's name and date (eg,Ashton 1989' or 'Clark 12 Jul 80') in your notes and at the top right corner of your record cards or sheets makes cross-referencing and retrieval easier. Figure 3 illustrates the record system.

Timing

A common mistake in student projects is to plunge straight into the detailed investigation without adequate conceptual equipment and a 'map' of the organization. Such rash approaches usually result in the investigation becoming bogged down. Valuable resources of time and goodwill are consumed and lost, and the field is muddied. Do not find yourself in the position of 'When all else fails read the instructions'. Do not panic because time is short: time given to the preparatory study of the concepts and the organization is well invested. Keep a close check on your timetable

Concept Review

On the concepts side the first step is to find out as much as possible about the knowledge area related to the issue, known as 'reviewing the literature', although this knowledge is not limited to published books. Sources of information include your own background experience and learning, periodicals and journals, the media, publications, documents and reports of organizations, people who work or have done research in the same area, and reports of similar investigations.

Other sources are experienced practitioners both outside and inside your organization, and information about proven 'best practice' in the field. In short you should seek every possible source from which to assemble as much knowledge as you can.

Many students fail to make full use of libraries, either because they are not familiar with library resources or because they think that searching in a library is difficult and time consuming. If you are not used to working in a library seek the advice and assistance of the professional librarians. They are not there just to check books out and in - that is the work of library assistants. Librarians are very well qualified in the art of tracing sources and cross-references. As professionals they are keen to use their skills. They can be very helpful in explaining how the library is organized and how to find books and articles on particular topics. In some cases they will even trace material and make up lists and abstracts. When you first go to a library ask to see one of the librarians and explain what your project is about. You should find that he or she is willing to help you to use the library effectively and quickly to trace material.

All public libraries have reference sections. Academic libraries and the libraries of professional institutions produce bibliographies for specific subjects. All libraries have photocopying facilities and can obtain virtually any publication temporarily through the national inter-library loan scheme. Most libraries are connected to computerised data banks.

A mistake many students make in using a book or publication about their project's subject is believing that they must read through the whole text and make detailed notes of it all. You should learn how to take an overview of a book and to dip into it for the relevant concepts. Use the list of contents and the index to find relevant parts and make notes or photocopies of just those parts. It is better to dip into a number of publications in the same subject area so that you get a wider view of appropriate concepts than just one writer would give you.

Remember that the purposes of your project are to extend your field of knowledge, to improve your skill in carrying out an investigation and to bring fresh light on to the particular issue. It is therefore vital that you reach out beyond the bounds of your present knowledge and beyond the bounds of the organization in which you are operating into a much wider field of knowledge and experience.

As you begin to assemble a selection of concepts you will find that you are stimulating ideas about models you might use and what you will want to look for in your preliminary survey of the organization.

You may find it useful to summarise your concepts and models with by putting them on paper in the form of `mind-maps`, like that shown in Figure 4. They have the advantage that you can revise and redraw them as your concept review proceeds.

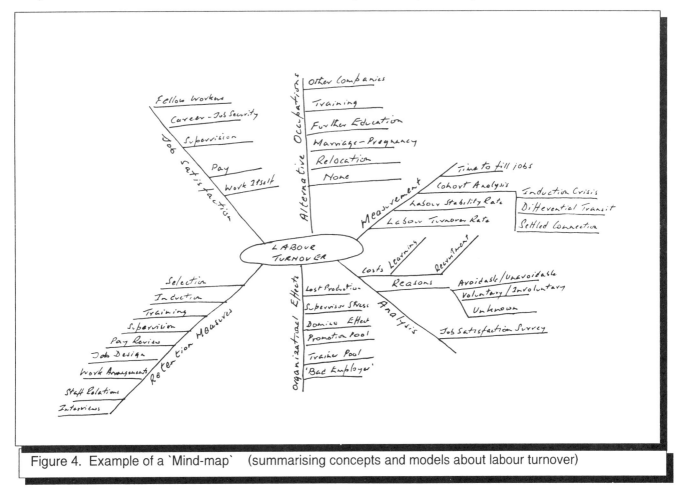

Figure 4. Example of a `Mind-map`   (summarising concepts and models about labour turnover)

Preliminary Survey of Organization

The first step on the evidence side is to build up a background picture of the factors affecting the issue in the organization. It is essential that you go to look at the place and to talk to the people involved. This may help you to understand the factors to be taken into account: history; economic, political, social, technological, legal and physical constraints; internal politics, power and relationships. You should sense the climate: what are the feelings and attitudes among managers, supervisors, employees and trade union representatives about the issues and the prospect of you intervening to enquire about the situation? Even if you have the agreement of senior management, or even if you are conducting the project within your own employing organization, you will be viewed with a degree of suspicion: individual members of the staff may have their own anxieties, jealousies and need for self-protection. Some may even be resentful that they have to spend precious time with you. People should be approached with care: if they see a threat in your activities they will not co-operate with you and may actively obstruct you. The issue must be placed in context as they see it: it may seem important to you and to the management who have agreed the project, but does it have any significance to the people whose help you seek and do they see any snags, objections and constraints that you have not allowed for? You may have to listen to gossip, but do not get involved in it.

During this survey you should gather information about the organization: 'who's who', reports on activities, publications about the aims and structure, organization charts, and the names, locations and telephone numbers of those individuals likely to be of help to you. If you can, you should find out what records of information they hold and which you would be allowed to consult. Whenever you visit the site, make notes of the information you gather. Immediately afterwards write up in you record system the information and impressions you have gained. While you are doing this preliminary survey you must try hard to keep an open mind: do not jump to conclusions about the resolution of the issue. Treat with caution the ready solutions some individuals in the organization may thrust upon you: they may be right because they have an intimate knowledge of the situation, but they may be wrong because of their restricted or biased view. Record their views for later analysis. You should also look out for leads on the concepts that will be appropriate to the issue in this situation.

Method of Investigation

Back on the concepts side you should now have a large array of concepts that could be appropriate to the issue. You will probably have too many to use immediately, so you will have to sort them out in order of importance and for immediate use. The remainder may become useful later or when you reach the conclusions stage of the investigation. At this point you should seek a model or models that can best illuminate and explain the issue and which identify the sort of evidence you will need to seek. From the selection of the models and the identification of the evidence needed you will then be able to construct a method by which you can investigate.

You may have begun to assemble some ideas about the methods that deploy the conceptual models and gather the evidence but before you jump in you should look at some of the literature on research methods used in your field of knowledge. Your librarian and your supervisor can help you to find useful publications. Examples of the literature available are given in the Bibliography at the end of Part 4. You might also consider the various computer software packages designed for particular fields of research, or consult tutors in the computer field about the programming of specific methods. Most valuable of all you may be able to find books or reports on investigations done on the same type of issue. All these will give you ideas about methods. You might find some previous project whose methods you wish to 'replicate'; this is quite legitimate but you will get more satisfaction and experience from designing some of your own methods.

There are a number of technical points to consider: is the use of a computer for analysis available and desirable; are the methods valid (obtaining the information actually needed) and reliable (eliminating unintended variables and measuring accurately); would sampling be a fair representation of the whole; how much time is needed and available; what methods of recording can be used; how can results be analysed (indigestible data is a little use)? Although a scientific approach to investigation emphasises the value of quantifying and measuring in collecting data, it is not always necessary to prove or disprove a point by figures, or statistical analysis, correlations and probabilities. Some studies are best done by such methods; some are better done with more open-ended observation and analysis; some benefit from a combination of quantifying and argued opinion. Some figures may clinch a point precisely, but too many may create a confusion that obscures the issue. You have to seek a balance appropriate to the issue.

Pilot Study

At this stage you should design your methods for collecting evidence, provisionally, and then try them out on a few people to see if they will work. This 'pilot study' will show up the unexpected snags, for example: people's misinterpretations of questions asked; misprints or omissions in paperwork; logistic difficulties of seeking and receiving information; inappropriateness of models; difficulties of recording and analysis of data. Many student projects receive severe setbacks because the investigation is launched without a pilot study and snags are met that cannot be rectified, or valuable time and co-operation is lost in going back to the beginning. Some form of pilot study is essential;

some investigators will even conduct several pilot studies, going back to the drawing board each time to refine the methods. The purposes of the project include persuading both the programme assessors and the organization's management that the issue has been expertly investigated: one acid test of an investigation is assessing the validity and reliability of the methods, and an investigation that fails that test has little credibility. A pilot study will enable you to get it right before you embark on the main fieldwork.

FIELD WORK

Sharpening Up

As a result of the preparatory study and the pilot study it will probably become apparent that there is a need to sharpen up your issue and plans. You may find that you need to re-define the issue and the aim of the investigation. You may find you have been over-ambitious for the time and resources available to you and you may need to narrow down the scope. You may find that the assumed problem has separated out into several clearer issues, or that the hypothesis is not precise enough for the people or material available for testing. You must continue to ask yourself: 'Have I identified the real problem?' or 'Is my hypothesis precise enough?'. There is no reason why you should not re-define or reduce the scope at this stage: it is more important to achieve a good quality end than to go on with a shallow and patchy investigation. Obviously, you would discuss any major change of direction or aim with your supervisor and the host organization. This may need some adjustment of your method design, but it is better to get it right now before you carry out your main enquiries.

Main Enquiry

The main enquiry into evidence should now be a straight-forward process, depending on good planning, logistics, administration and some luck. Particularly important is the preparation of materials and notifying people well in advance. If no snags arise it may not take much time and may even seem an anticlimax to you. That could prove the thoroughness of your planning and preparation. But unexpected snags arise often though: people you expected to talk to are not available; documents cannot be found; material by mail is delayed; some information you receive proves to require yet other material to support it. Some contingency planning is advisable to cope with delays and dead ends. You should be able to fall back on alternative or parallel methods of enquiry, alternative people to interview or consult, or secondary sources of information. Some gaps in data may be unavoidable; follow-up studies to fill the gaps depend on the time left, the importance of the data and people's tolerance. Few enquiries end up without some of the measurements spoiled, or some data lost, or some questionnaires not returned. You must allow time in the planning of the enquiry for snags and delays: if none arise you will have

more time for the remaining stages. You should have a detailed timetable for your fieldwork. If you are familiar with the techniques of networks and bar charts you could use one of these methods for your planning and progress. At the least you should keep a list of tasks with target dates and a log of their completion.

Withdrawal

A halt must be called to the fieldwork at some point. The law of diminishing returns probably applies and you need a considerable amount of time to synthesize all the concepts and evidence you have assembled for your evaluation, conclusions, and recommendations, and then to write up your report. In many ways it is better for you to withdraw completely from the organization at this point, except for services essential for the report. If you stand right away from the situation in the field you can concentrate better on the concepts and evidence you have assembled. If you keep going back to the field to follow new leads or fine points or improvements in data you will eat up the essential time left for the remaining stages of the project and you may not be able to 'see the wood for the trees'.

SYNTHESIS
EVALUATION

Relevant Concepts and Models

By this stage you will have decided which of the concepts you have assembled are really relevant and useful to the issue and the evidence you have collected. Your familiarity with them over a period of time probably has helped you to interrelate them and build you own models that you can apply to the evidence to evaluate it. You should write down your concepts and arrange them on paper into suitable categories or models. The more you commit them to paper in statements or diagrams the more you will refine and select them. Remember that you must justify the concepts in your report: explain them to yourself on paper and throw out those that you cannot explain or that are not used to evaluate evidence. Confused or redundant concepts in your report will weaken your credibility.

Summarising Evidence

You will have assembled a great deal of evidence by now. It could include financial and numerical data, expressed opinions, survey results, identified constraints and future plans. It needs to be set out, categorised and analysed. Again it is best to manipulate it on paper: write it down in statements, tables and diagrams; arrange it and re-arrange it to see if you can discern relationships and trends; try to match it up with your concepts. This writing and re-writing is not wasted as it will help you to establish relationships and present it in such a way that you can explain it in your report. It will enable you to decide which facts are important and which are not. Some of the tables and figures you produce will be useful for incorporation in your report. You do not have to use all the facts you have assembled in evidence, only those that are relevant and significant. In your report you should not present evidence that cannot be matched up with concepts to throw light on the issue.

Implications

As you relate your chosen concepts to their appropriate evidence you should be able to draw from each set the implications of the facts, for example: patterns, trends and relationships that give indications for the future; efficiencies or deficiencies in processes and practices; attainable or unattainable objectives; myths and misinterpretions about the situation; gaps in knowledge and records; false assumptions; relative costs and benefits. It is important that you treat each concepts+evidence=implications set separately at this stage so that you are not tempted to draw out more implications from the concept and evidence than they together justify. To do so would destroy your credibility for critical analysis. Again, you should write out these sets in such a way that you can explain and present them. Think about how you would incorporate them in your reports. You may be able to prepare diagrams and tables that will slot into the report eventually. Do not expect the outcome of your evaluation to be instantaneous. You will need a period of gestation during which you can manipulate the concepts and evidence: the longer you can think about them, the more accurate will be the implications you draw out.

CONCLUSIONS

What the Overall Situation Is.

By now you have assembled a number of implications deduced from your enquiry, some related, some apparently independent. You cannot use or present them in this state: your task now is to bring them together like pieces of a jigsaw puzzle to produce an overall picture of the situation, as it relates to the issue. That could mean that you may have to throw away some, as not part of this particular picture. To bring the implications together in the right relationship may need the application of other concepts, and you must be prepared to explain such concepts if you use them. In stating what the overall situation is, you are forming your expert opinion. This must be founded on the investigation you have made so far, on the concepts deployed, evidence found and implications deduced. You cannot at this late stage drag in opinions unsupported by the evidence and concepts: to do so would destroy the credibility of your diagnosis.

What Could Happen As A Result

Based on your opinion of the current situation related to the issue, you can now consider what could happen if that situation were allowed to continue untreated. To do so you may need more concepts, which will have to be explained, but again you must be careful to build on

the solid ground of your diagnosis in making this prognosis. The prognosis is a key element in the conclusions of a report: with the diagnosis it forms the persuasive base from which you can project your possible courses of action and your recommendations

What Could Be Done About It.

You can now begin to deal with the issue by considering a number of possible alternative actions that individually or collectively could resolve it. You do not jump straight to a solution; you follow the rational process of decision-making by first searching for and exploring all the possible options open to you. You obviously need more conceptual support here, to be explained if used. In exploring each option you have a duty to take into account any constraining factors, to estimate or predict the likely outcomes in terms of costs and benefits, or disadvantages and advantages, or risks and probabilities, or constraints and opportunities. You should also consider the practical problems of implementing the action. In an imaginative way you could come up with a vast number of options, but you have to see them in the context of the organization's reality and therefore you may need to prune them down to those that are realistic possibilities. You may have to come to the conclusion that for some or all aspects of the issue there are no possible solutions, beyond further investigation. This is legitimate but if you decide this be sure that you have considered it seriously. You will see that the conclusions stage represents a substantial part of the investigation and again your credibility is at stake. It needs its own period of time for analysis and synthesis and should not be rushed. In the report it will have a most significant and substantial part to play in persuading the assessor and the manager.

RECOMMENDATIONS

What Should Be Done

In the conclusions you have explored what 'could' be done. You are now going to stick out your neck and state what 'should' be done. If you have considered the various options thoroughly you simply have to select your 'best buys' from among them. You cannot introduce any other options at this stage, nor can you build into a particular course of action any conditions that were not included in the conclusions considerations. You should be able to state each recommendation separately and concisely as a specific action to be taken. Amplification and discussion about each will have been covered in the conclusions.

Check

Your recommendations will be subject to the greatest critical scrutiny. You should question yourself about each point and make sure that the answer is satisfactory:

- To what extent do they resolve the issue?

- To what extent do they achieve the aim?

- Is each supported by the evidence?

- Is each explained in the Conclusions under `what could be done about it'?

- Is each acceptable in the light of the organization's climate?

- Are they practicable with the organization's external and internal constraints?

- Are the methods of carrying them out considered?

- Do the benefits outweigh the costs in financial and human terms, in the short and long terms?

Your purpose in the end is to influence your assessor and the organization. Your persuasiveness will depend on the importance of the issue, your knowledge displayed in the concepts, your skill and thoroughness in seeking the evidence, the critical nature of your evaluation, the soundness of your conclusions and the practicality of your recommendations - all of which you will have to demonstrate in your report.

PERSUASION

The Conclusions and the Recommendations together follow the age-old model of persuasion used by politicians, consultants, advertisers, salesmen and con-men to persuade others to accept or buy something:

1. First, reveal to the subject that he or she has a problem or opportunity to gain something, playing on anxieties or desires (or fear or greed) (what the situation is).

2. Next, heighten the subject's anxiety or desires by emphasising what would happen if the problem or opportunity is not grasped (what could happen as a result).

3. Next, explore with the subject a number of possible actions that could resolve the problem or gain the desired object, identifying in each the possible costs and benefits. (The unscrupulous may introduce some bias here by omitting or over-emphasising some aspects) (what could be done about it).

4. Finally, clinch the transaction by recommending, from 3 above, the actions that would obviously be the most advantageous to the subject (what should be done about it).

Stages	Approximate proportion of time
ARRANGING PROJECT	1/5th
1. ISSUE	
Choice of Topic	
Agreement of Issue and Aim with Host Organization	
PREPARATORY STUDY	1/5th
2. CONCEPTS 3. EVIDENCE	
Concept Review	
Preliminary Survey of Organization	
Method of Investigation	
Pilot Study	
FIELD WORK	1/5th
Sharpening up	
Main Enquiry	
Withdrawal	
SYNTHESIS	1/5th
4. EVALUATION	
Relevant Concepts Summarising & Models Evidence	
Drawing Implications	
5. CONCLUSIONS	
What the Overall Situation Is (Diagnosis) What Could Happen as a Result (Prognosis) What Could be Done about It (Possible Treatments)	
6. RECOMMENDATIONS	
What Should be Done about it (Chosen Treatments)	
REPORT	1/5th
Drafting	
Final Report	

Figure 5. Sequence & Timing of a Project

AIM

The aim of the investigation was to resolve the issue. Your report has a different aim: to persuade your assessor that you have developed the right level of expertise and to persuade the management of the host organization to accept your findings and recommendations. You would be wise therefore to have the structure of a report in mind right from the beginning of the project because it is the end product by which you will stand or fall, and because it will help you to plan and design your investigation more effectively.

Your report has to carry the reader right through the investigation process, as you have conducted and refined it:

- In the title and introduction you have to set the scene by giving just enough background information about the organization and its history for your particular readers will require to understand the context, by defining the issue as a problem or opportunity hypothesis, and by stating the aim of the investigation (not the aim of the report).

- In the main sections of the report you then have to explain the concepts that you have chosen to use, the methods you devised to seek the necessary evidence, and the evidence itself. Also in those sections you will have to show what implications you drew out from each combination of concepts and evidence as you evaluated one against the other.

- In the conclusions you need to draw together all your findings to express your opinion, based on what you have set out in the main sections and in relation to the issue, what the overall situation is, what could happen as a result, and what actions could be taken to resolve the issue.

- In the recommendations you set out what actions should be taken, selected from 'what actions could be taken' in the conclusions.

There must be a continuous thread running through the report, connecting the issue and aim at the beginning, through the concepts, evidence and evaluation, to the conclusions and recommendations at the end. Everything in the report must be relevant to, and justified by, that thread.

CONVENTIONS

You could structure the report in any way that takes your fancy, but in the persuasion game you must take into account your readers' expectations and the perceptions they will have of you and your investigation from the report. Your significant readers are the assessor and the organization's managers. You would be wise therefore to present the report in the format that they would expect, in a legible, logical and business-like narrative and with an appearance of care and quality. The format I have recommended so far meets the expectations of most academic institutions and most organizations. You can choose to use a different format but be sure that it will meet the rationale and quality standards of the recommended one if you are to avoid an unfavourable comparison.

The style of writing is important as it also affects the reader's assumptions about you and your level of expertise:

- Do not write in note form. Use complete sentences (ie beginning with a capital letter, ending with a fullstop and, normally, containing a verb).

- Avoid long-winded sentences, slang and unnecessary jargon.

- If you use abbreviations always give the full words the first time you use them.

- Decide on a comprehensive hierarchy of headings, appropriate to the size of the report. Use it consistently throughout the report to give it a structure and to provide the reader with headline guides. Too many headings are preferable to too few.

- Break your text up into reasonable sized paragraphs and sub-paragraphs.

- Use a thesaurus to seek alternative words and to check your spelling.

Within the format structure there are many conventions that are set out in detail in Part 5 and are illustrated in the example report in Part 6. The conventions have evolved to serve purposes of structure, ease of reading and reference, and logical presentation. Again, you can express your individuality by ignoring these conventions. If you choose to substitute others, again be sure that they achieve the same purposes if you want to avoid irritating the readers whom you wish to persuade of your expertise.

Some academic institutions may specify some variations to the conventions shown: if your institution does so you must of course incorporate their requirements.

DRAFTING

The greatest difficulty in composing a report is inertia: great efforts of willpower are needed to start it and follow it through, and make it all hang together. You have some idea of the structure now, and you will have assembled a lot of material that can go into the report. But you cannot sit down and write a report straight off like a 'Dear Mum' letter. You need a plan and you need to go through a constructing and drafting process. To overcome the inertia and to keep the overall structure under control I recommend this process:

1. First, make a 'blueprint' as your overall guide. Set out on one large piece of paper (stuck on a wall if necessary) the headings of all the major sections or chapters you propose to use in the report. Check these with the section 'Format of a Report - Content & Sequence' in Part 5.

2. On the same sheet, pencil in under the section or chapter headings all the group and paragraph headings that seem appropriate. Headings of tables, figures and appendices can be slotted in. The report can be seen as a whole now; keep it before you and amend and augment it as you proceed with the drafting.

3. Now put each heading on a separate sheet of A4 paper in a loose leaf folder and fill in on each sheet the notes and data relevant to it. Previously prepared tables, figures and appendices can be slotted into the folder. The report is now beginning to take shape and it is possible to modify the structure and content distribution to get the balance and sequence right. Cross-check it frequently with the 'blueprint'.

4. Next, re-write each sheet in turn in full narrative form, modifying, selecting and pruning the notes and data available on the original sheet. Write legibly so that the sheets can be read as a draft by your supervisor and can be copied easily by a typist for the final report. Be precise in laying out the format, type of headings, spelling and punctuation. Do not assume that the typist will construct and polish your report to meet all the conventions. If major modifications to the report become necessary after discussion with your supervisor this system will make it easy to re-arrange sheets or re-write parts.

5. Finally, go through the whole report, checking the thread, pruning and correcting.

You will see that this system makes a continuous build-up possible, overcomes the inertia and is always under control. The process is also fairly quick. When the draft is complete, agree it with you supervisor before having any of it typed into the final report.

You may have access to a personal computer and a word processing facility. This can make the task easier. Material can be amended and moved about. During the drafting stage you will find it more flexible and manageable if you keep each chapter, major section, appendix and large table on separate `files` or `documents` on the computer. They will be easier to amend and you can print them out in sequence for the final report.

LENGTH

The expected length of the report is usually specified by the programme tutors, according to the level and importance of the project in the qualification. It is often stated as 'between x thousand and y thousand words of original text'.'Original text' means that which you have composed or re-written in your own words: copies of others' documents or printed text would not be counted. An assignment paper might be 1,000 to 2,000 words, an advanced or postgraduate diploma project report could be 5,000 to 10,000, a taught master's project report 10,000 to 20,000, and for higher research degrees the range would be proportionately higher. The difficulty is not in having enough to write; there is usually an abundance of material and the greatest difficulty is in boiling it down to the required length. Some tutors and many managers would argue that an essential skill in report writing is the ability to economise in words and to produce a concise report within the limits set; they might wish to make that a factor in assessment.

FINAL REPORT

You can produce your final report in manuscript, especially if it is at the assignment level. If you do so you must use the format and conventions and you must emulate the typist in neatness, legibility and appearance. However, most projects will require a typed final report, probably with several copies. Typing, reproduction and any binding take time and are expensive. Make sure that you allow for these in planning your project to meet the deadline.

The example report in Part 6 can be used to guide the typist in arranging the structure and layout according to the conventions. Many students now have access to a computer and word processor. This makes the compilation of the report easier. Parts can be drafted and changed easily as the project proceeds and a final print-out can be photocopied to produce satisfactory copies of the report.

ORAL REPORT

If you are required to make an oral presentation to augment your written report, you should base it on the highlights of the written report and follow the same sequence and structure in the presentation.

- When you have identified the highlights you should decide which of them would be better spoken and which would be better shown visually. For the former you need notes, for the latter carefully prepared flip-charts or overhead projector transparencies.

- Prepare and develop your notes as guidelines, not to be read verbatim but to enable you to say in your own spontaneous words the main points of the report. They should also indicate the points at which you will use your visual displays.

- Take advice on the preparation of visuals, and beware of cluttering them up with too much detail that would distract the audience. If you have to show a lot visually, use a number of simple and clear charts or transparencies.

- Decide too, for your specific audience, how long the presentation should take, including time for questions. A common fault is to make it too long.

- Just as the written report should flow smoothly along, so the oral presentation should hold the attention of the audience by being to the point and in logical steps.

- Before the final event have a rehearsal with a friendly but critical colleague.

- Immediately before the presentation check and double-check your notes, material and equipment..

- Speak clearly and confidently - you are the master of this particular subject.

CHECKLIST FOR ASSESSMENT OF AN INVESTIGATION AND THE REPORT

	Not adequate ✓	Just adequate ✓	Competent ✓	Excellent ✓	Remarks
1. ISSUE Clarity of background information					
Statement of problem or opportunity (hypothesis)					
Statement of the Aim of the Investigation					
2. CONCEPTS Wisdom in the use of relevant theories and/or academic knowledge					
Wisdom in the use of current `good practice , expertise and experience					
3. EVIDENCE Methods for observation and/or search for evidence relevant to the Issue					
Selection, description, analysis and organization of data and facts.					
4. EVALUATION Critical evaluation of the Evidence about the Issue, in the light of related Concepts,					
Implications drawn from Concepts-Evidence sets					
5. CONCLUSIONS Plausibility of opinions, supported by the Implications: `What the overall situation really is `(Diagnosis)					
`What **could** happen as a result` (Prognosis)					
`What **could** be done about it` (Possible Treatments)					
6. RECOMMENDATIONS `What **should** be done` in Costs (Recommended Treatment) to deal with the Issue in Practicability Feasibility in Acceptability					
7. PRESENTATION Quality of structure and organization of material					
Use of conventions					
Visual impact					
Flow of language, information and argument					
8. OVERALL ASSESSMENT Credibility and effectiveness of the investigation and the report. **(NOT an average of 1-7)**					

BIBLIOGRAPHY FOR PARTS 1 - 4

ACKROYD S & J A HUGHES 1981 *Data collection in context* London: Longmans. Concentrates on social survey and interviews, and participant observation. Considers the wider social and cultural factors which affect the intellectual authority of methods.

BARRY R 1994 *The research project: how to write it* London: Routledge. Practical advice.

BELL J 1987 *Doing a research project* Milton Keynes: Open University Press. A guide to first-time research in education and social science. Useful in literature search and the collection of evidence.

BENNETT R 1979 *Using research in training* Bradford: MCB Ltd (JEIT Monograph). Gives useful guidelines on how research can be used, what research is, the various methods and techniques of research, with some interesting examples.

BUZAN T 1989 *Use your head* BBC Publications. Useful advice on memory and studying.

CAMERON S 1994 *The MBA handbook - essential study skills* 2nd Edn London: Pitman. Has useful chapters on report writing and projects, theses and dissertations, especially choice of topic and data collection.

CROSTHWAITE E 1993 *Passing your IPM exams.* London; Institute of Personnel Management. Has a chapter on the management report required for IPM (now IPD) professional qualification.

HOWARD K & J A SHARP 1983 *The management of a student research project* Aldershot: Gower. Good on literature search and collection of data.

KANE E 1985 *Doing your own research* Marion Boyer. Basic ideas.

LEEDY P D 1995 *Practical research: planning and design* London: Macmillan.

LUMLEY J S P & W BENJAMIN 1994 *Research: some ground rules* Oxford University Press. As title.

MACKENZIE DAVEY D, D ROCKINGHAM GILL & P McDONNELL 1970 *Attitude surveys in industry: IPM information report 3* London: Institute of Personnel Management. Basic advice on objectives and methods of attitude surveying, with a number of case studies in organizations.

PREECE R 1994 *Starting research* London: Pinter. Gives basic ideas but also carries subject into advanced research for academic dissertaions and theses. Comrehensive and detailed.

McCROSSAN L 1984 *A handbook for interviewers* London: HMSO. An excellent guide produced by the Social Survey Division of the government Office of Population Censuses and Surveys, based on many years of experience of interviewing the public.

MAXWELL A E 1970 *Basic statistics in behavioural research* Harmondsworth: Penguin. A beginner's guide, biased towards pyschology, but with useful advice.

MORGAN G (Ed) 1983 *Beyond method: strategies for social research* London: Sage Publications. Readings by a number of leading researchers.

MOORE N 1983 *How to do research* London: The Library Association. A practical guide, written mainly from experience in library information research but covering all aspects from the setting the objective to the written report and dissemination.

OPPENHEIM A N 1968 *Questionnaire design and attitude measurement* London: Heinemann. Very readable on both aspects. Deals well with wording of statements and questions, quantifying questionnaire data, checklists, semantic differential and rating scales, and evaluation research.

PHILLIPS E & D S PUGH 1987 *How to get a PhD* Milton Keynes: Open University Press. Managing the peaks and troughs of research, specifically for PhD.

SPECTOR P E 1981 *Research designs* London: Sage Publications. Deals particularly with quantitative methods in social sciences research.

SUDMAN S & N M BRADBURN 1982 *Asking questions: a practical guide to questionnaire design* London: Jossey-Bass. Comprehensive text on questionnaires, using examples from a wide range of surveys in various fields of knowledge.

TURABIAN K L 1982 *A manual for writers of research papers, theses and dissertations* London: Heinemann. As the title states.

WATSON G 1987 *Writing a thesis - a guide to long essays and dissertations* London: Longmans.

STUDENT REPORT WRITING

1.   This part of the Guide describes and illustrates the format and conventions of report writing for students. It is set out as it might be produced on a typewriter or on a word processor and the right margin is not justified.

2.   Some educational or professional institutions specify their requirements for reports, theses and dissertations for the award of their qualifications.   The guidance given here conforms to the British Standard recommendations for the presentation of theses and dissertations - BS 4821/1990, which has been agreed by the major library and university authorities in the United Kingdom.

3.   The format and conventions used in this guide cover adequately the needs for most assignments and reports for diplomas, first degrees and taught higher degrees.   Students preparing theses and dissertations for research degrees will need some additional guidance available in BS4821:1990 or in a more detailed guide such Preece or Turabian in the Bibliography above.

FORMAT OF A REPORT - CONTENT & SEQUENCE

4.   A report contains each of the following sections or chapters, each beginning on a new page, in the sequence shown below. Only those printed bold are essential in any report and may be enough for a short report. The rest are optional extras that can be added in their places in the sequence of a larger report.

TITLE PAGE - the details of author, purpose of submission and date.

ACKNOWLEDGEMENTS - to those who have assisted the author in the investigation.

ABSTRACT - a summary of the whole report on one page (may be called SUMMARY).

CONTENTS - giving page numbers.

INTRODUCTION - the background, the issue and the aim of the investigation.

METHOD - used in the investigation.

MAJOR SECTIONS - as many as necessary, usually covering the concepts used, the evidence collected and the evaluation.

CONCLUSIONS - overall findings of the investigation: the overall picture that has emerged and the implications; possible course of actions, with costs, benefits and constraints.

RECOMMENDATIONS - actions that should be taken, based on the Conclusions.

APPENDICES - bulky material supporting but not essential to the text.

REFERENCES - identification of literature and other sources used and referred to in the text.

BIBLIOGRAPHY - other literature related to the investigation but not referred to in the text.

The purposes and conventions of each of these sections are dealt with below.

TITLE PAGE

5.   The Title page, which can act also as the front cover in a short report, has spaced out in descending order:

a.   The title in bold block capitals at the top centre. The title in itself is a summary of the report: it needs to be concise yet able to attract the reader and distinguish it from other reports.

b.   The author's full name. Copyright may be stated by placing © before the author`s name.

c.   The qualification for which the report is submitted.

d.   The institution or organization to which the report is submitted.

e.   The month and year of submission.

ACKNOWLEDGEMENTS

6.   The Acknowledgements page enables the author to express thanks to those who have helped with the project and the report, giving title and name, job title and organization.

ABSTRACT

7.   The Abstract is a summary of the whole report - the background and purposes of the project, the methods used, the main findings, the conclusions and recommendations, and reference to any related reports. It has two purposes. It provides the busy reader with an overview of the whole report. It can also be taken from the report as a document in its own right for reference purposes. It is restricted to a single page of A4 and therefore demands strict editing. In reports designed mainly for an organization, rather than an academic institution, it can be called the Summary.

CONTENTS

8.   The Contents page or pages list, for the whole report, the main sections and any important sub-sections with the page numbers. In a very long or complex report further lists may be given of tables, figures and illustrations, with their page numbers.

INTRODUCTION

9.   The Introduction sets the scene for the reader and motivates him or her to read the report. It includes enough background information, the issue to be investigated, and the aim of the investigation. It looks forward and therefore does not contain reference to any material in the sections that follow. Its main components are shown below in the sequence they are presented. They can be used as headings within the Introduction.

10.   **Background.** The reader is given enough information about the history and circumstances to enable him or her to understand the organization concerned and the issue that has been identified. The quantity of material will be decided by the persons who will use the report. Those inside the organization may require little background information: those outside may require a lot.

11.   **Issue.** The project must have a reason. It will be focused on a particular issue that requires investigation. It may be a problem that faces the organization, for which a solution is desired. On the other hand it may be that the organization has identified a potential opportunity for benefit and wants it to be investigated. Such opportunities are usually phrased as `If we did so-and-so, such-and-such benefits would result`. or `Our procedure for so-and-so could be improved.`. These are hypotheses to be tested out by an investigation, possibly with some implementation to follow.

12.   **Aim of the Investigation.** The aim of the investigation has to be stated as the final point of the Introduction, to enable the reader to know what the investigator sought to do to resolve the issue and to recommend actions. It should be noted that it is distinct from the aim of the report, which is persuade the reader to accept the findings and recommendations of the investigator.

METHOD

13.   The methods used in the investigation can be stated in this section to enable the reader to appreciate and assess the stringency and thoroughness with which the author sought out the evidence to match the concepts used. It would include people and places visited, measuring devices designed and used, pilot studies and questionnaires. Some of the material of this section could be consigned to appendices, with just the main points made in the section.

14.   If serious obstacles prevented the investigator from making some enquiries these should be stated in the Method section so that the reader will understand why some aspects were not fully explored.

MAJOR SECTIONS

15.   The main body of the report is divided into major sections for a short report, or chapters for longer reports. There is no specific format for this part of the report but it should be given a logical and persuasive structure that will lead the reader to the point when conclusions can be revealed. For example succeeding sections could be devoted to the concepts brought to bear on the investigation, the evidence found, and then the evaluation. Alternatively each section might deal with one set of concepts, evidence and evaluation. It is up to the author to decide the best structure.

16.   As it is necessary to carry the reader through smoothly the text should be kept as concise as possible, with the essential and important discussion. To help this, detailed information can be assigned to appendices but it is important that the essential information is given in the text. If the reader is forced to turn to an appendix to follow the thread of the account the author has distributed the information badly.

CONCLUSIONS

17.   The Conclusions section or chapter of the report draws on the evidence, argument and facts set out in the Introduction and Main Sections. It cannot introduce new evidence or factual material but some new concepts may be introduced to bring together the various findings and implications. If the previous parts have been constructed clearly and logically the conclusions will follow naturally from them, maintaining the persuasive thread.

18.   The language should be simple and direct and if a number of major points are to be made they should be set out in separate paragraphs. If need be, reference can be made back to previous text by page number and paragraph.

19.   A report is part of a decision-making process. Sometimes a report may end at the Conclusions, leaving others to decide the appropriate course of action. The Conclusions themselves must be persuasive therefore.

20.   In simple terms it is the function of the Conclusions to give the author's expert opinion about the Issue, based on the Concepts, Evidence and Evaluation set out in the previous sections. The Conclusions should state:

   a.   What the overall situation is (diagnosis).

   b.   What could happen as a result if the situation continues untreated (prognosis)

   c.   What could be done about it - possible courses of action, spelling out for each:
   the constraints, possible outcomes, costs and benefits (possible treatment).

Note that the word `could` is used in the prognosis and possible treatments: the word `should` is reserved for Recommendations.

RECOMMENDATIONS

21.   Recommendations are usually required.   The important principles are:

   a.   They must be restricted to selections from the possible courses of action set out in the Conclusions, para 20c above.

   b.   They cannot introduce any new material.

   c.   They should state concisely and precisely what `should` be done to resolve the Issue.

   d.   They should be set out in sentences (not note-form) and in separate paragraphs, which should be numbered for ease of reference.

APPENDICES

22.   Supporting documents and detailed information are assigned the annotation `APPENDIX A`, APPENDIX B`, etc in the order to which they are referred to in the text.  In the text this would be indicated by `see Appendix A`. If original documents such as questionnaires, forms, maps, pictures or reports are to be appendices they must conform to the A4 paper size of the report. Photocopying can be used to increase or decrease documents to A4.

23.   An appendix written specifically for the report is set out in the same way as the rest of the text, with heading and paragraphs. It begins on a new page and has its own title heading at top centre. `APPENDIX    ` is placed at top right of the page.   The page numbers follow on from the page numbers of the preceding sections of the report.

24.   If the appendix is an original document `APPENDIX    ` is added at top right and the page numbers are added.

25.   Original documents that are not A4 in size must be photocopied or folded down to A4. If they are smaller they must be photocopied up to A4 or mounted on A4 paper.

26.   As with tables and diagrams appendices should be laid out in a vertical format (ie portrait, not landscape) so that the reader can consult them without having to rotate the report.   Oversize folded documents should also fold out to be read without having to rotate the report.

REFERENCES

27.   The References section sets out, in an accepted convention, the literature and other sources that support statements and quotations made in the text.   This gives the reader opportunity to verify those statements and quotations by consulting the references.   More details are given in the Source Materials and Referencing sections below.

BIBLIOGRAPHY

28.   The Bibliography section is sometimes introduced if the author wishes to give the reader information about other literature and source material that are related to the subject of the investigation but are not referred to in the text. It should not be confused with References.   It is set out in the same format as the References section.

CONVENTIONS OF REPORT WRITING

29.   The conventions set out below are designed to ease reference, reading and understanding. They are as specified in British Standard BS 4821/1990 which has been up-dated from the previous BS4821/1972. Most are used in this part of the Guide and are illustrated in the example report in Part 6.

APPEARANCE AND LAYOUT

30.   **Paper.** The report should be typed, or printed from a word processor, on white A4 paper, 70-100gsm weight, on one side (recto) only, and in the vertical `portrait` format.

31.   **Type.** Characters should be not less than 2mm high for capitals and not less than 1.5mm for the lower case x.   This page is printed to that standard, using 10 point characters.

32.   **Spacing.** Lines are at one-and-a-half spacing (although double spacing may be used). Where in normal typing a space would be left, as between paragraphs and above and below headings, the report spacing is doubled so that the gap between paragraphs and above and below headings will be three spaces in one-and-a-half spacing (and four in double spacing).

33.   **Margins.** The left hand margin should be at least 40mm and all others at least 15mm.

34.   **Line Length.** Lines should contain 60-90 characters, counting a space between words as a character.

35.   **Chapters.** Each chapter (or main section in a short report) should be numbered, have a heading and start on a new page.

36.   **Indenting.** Indenting should be between 5mm and 10mm.

37.   **Page Numbering.** Page numbers should begin counting the title page as page 1, but the number 1 is not shown on the title page.   The page numbers continue through the report, including all appendices, references and bibliography sections. Page numbers preferably should be placed at the top right corner of the page, using Arabic numbers 1,2, 3 , etc.

38.   **Headings.** Headings serve two purposes in the report: to act as a guide for the reader and to give the author a disciplined framework in which to write. The author must decide the optimum use of headings but a report without headings is difficult to read or refer back to. This part uses a lot of headings, to illustrate but also to ease reference to the contents. Although headings are to guide the reader, readers often do not read them but go straight to the text. For this reason a heading should be seen, like a heading in a newspaper, as distinct from the text. It should not be part of the sentence. An acid test is to blot out the headings to see if the text still makes sense. Try:

`Head Office. This is located in the centre of the city away from the plant.`

39.   **Hierarchy of Headings.** A hierarchy of headings indicates the beginning of four different divisions of the text: a chapter, a major section, a group of paragraphs, a paragraph or a sub-paragraph. Each has a specific style and/or position in relation to the text. Not more than four different types should be used. A hierarchy of three types is recommended, they can be seen in this part and in Part 6:

a.   **Main or Centre Headings.** The largest spanning heading is used to indicate the chapters and major sections. It is in bold block capitals and is placed centrally on the. page.

b.   **Group Headings.** The next, lower, heading indicates a further sub-division of a chapter or major section. It controls one or more paragraphs. It is also in bold block capitals but is placed at the left-hand margin.

c.   **Paragraph and Sub-paragraph Headings.** At the lowest level paragraphs and sub-paragraphs can be given their own headings, but they can be used only to control the text within their paragraph or sub-paragraph. They must not be part of the first sentence (see para 38 above). They are in bold lower case lettering with initial capital letters and are followed by a fullstop.

Older manual and electric typewriters do not have a bold facility: underlining can be used instead of bold. Some authors underline or embolden words or phrases within the text to emphasise them. This can be counter-productive and is not to be recommended as it distracts the reader from reading systematically and may result in some important points being missed.

40.   **Paragraphs.** There is no optimum length for a paragraph: it contains related matter but if it is too long the thread may be lost; if it is too short the effect may be staccato in appearance and reading. The initial word or paragraph number should begin at the margin - it is not indented. A paragraph may be given a heading (see para 39c above) but once paragraph headings are introduced each succeeding paragraph should be given a heading until the next superior heading occurs.

41.   **Sub-paragraphs.** Sub-paragraphs can be used to:

a.   Break up the flow of a very long paragraph.

b.   Tabulate a number of items or points.

A paragraph can continue after sub-paragraphing but only one set of sub-paragraphs may be used in a paragraph, to avoid confusion in referencing. Sub-paragraphs are indented in from the left margin and are usually lettered `a`, `b`, `c`, etc. Some authors bracket the letters, `(a)`, `(b)`, etc, but it is not necessary as the letters are distinct from the numbers. If it is necessary to introduce sub-sub-paragraphs they can be numbered `(1)`, `(2)`, `(3)`,etc. (Some authors use a hierarchy of decimal numbers for paragraphs and sub-paragraphs, for example: `1`, `1.1`,`1.2` , `1.1.1`, with or without indenting, but many readers find them confusing). The advice on the use of headings for paragraphs (see para 40 above) applies to sub-paragraph headings.

42.   **Additional Spacing.** A blank line space is left after each Main and Group heading and between paragraphs and sub-paragraphs. In one-and-a-half spacing the gap would be three spaces. (In double spacing it would be four spaces).

43.   **Numbering.** Some academics object to paragraph numbering on aesthetic grounds. The paragraphs have been numbered in this part to demonstrate the value for cross-reference and locating in a report. A simple method is to number paragraphs in Arabic `1`,`2`,`3`, etc, right from the first paragraph of the Introduction (not the Abstract or Summary), and continuing the numbers through the chapters and sections. Many government reports use this system. Chapters should be numbered `1`,`2`,`3`,etc, beginning with Chapter 1 - Introduction. It is not usual to number main headings or group headings within chapters.

44.   **Numbers.** Numbers are usually Arabic numerals but to avoid confusion the numbers 1 to 10 may be spelled out as `one`, `two`, etc. Numbers can also be spelled out to avoid mis-interpretation, eg `twenty  6 inch nails`.   Roman numerals take up space and are not understood by all.

45.   **Dates.** Dates are usually written in the style `12 April 1995` or `12 Apr 95`.

46.   **Quotations.** Verbatim quotations from other sources in the text should be placed within single quotation marks: quotations within them should then use double quotation marks. Large extracts quoted in the text should be indented   completely as a separate paragraph or paragraphs.

47.   **Footnotes.** `Footnotes are an interference with the flow of reading.  Such `side-glances` are better placed in brackets within the text or assigned to appendices.

48.   **Abbreviations.** Readers are irritated by abbreviations that are unfamiliar to them. If there is any doubt the full word or words should be used the first time with the abbreviation immediately after in brackets, eg, `Standard Operating Procedure  (SOP)`. It is now common practice to eliminate fullstops with abbreviations, eg, `TUC`, `T B Smith`, `10cm`.

STYLE OF WRITING

49.   Simple, clear and unambiguous language aids reading. Long-winded sentences, confused statements, unknown jargon and mis-spelling hinder and irritate and may damage the credibility of the author of a report. Complete grammatical sentences should be used always. Note-form or non-sentences may be interpreted as a lack of command of the language.   Useful guidance on style of writing can be found in Ernest Gowers ` Complete Plain Words` (Gowers 1987).   A thesaurus (eg, Roget 1990) is useful for spelling and alternative words.   Text should be pruned to eliminate unnecessary additional adjectives, extra phrases and explanatory sentences, especially in the drafting stage. The author is responsible for the accuracy of the final report. It is prudent therefore to have the report `proof-read` by another person before releasing it.

50.   In the past it was conventional for authors to refer to themselves in the text as `the author`, rather than `I` or `me`. Although sounding impartial it is often seen as pretentious. An impersonal style is better. For example: instead of `I saw that...` `It was seen that..`; instead of `The manager told me..` `The manager stated that..`.

SOURCE MATERIALS

51.   If the author is using theories, opinions, statements, facts, data, statistics, diagrams or other material that are not of his or her own creation he or she should be prepared to allow the reader to evaluate them by going to the original source. Also, courtesy demands that one should not use other people's ideas without acknowledgement. It is also prudent to check if an individual`s personal statements or an organization`s information is free from confidentiality before using them. To avoid embarrassment to an individual it may be appropriate to de-personalise the information, eg: `one manager said that.....` The conventions for acknowledging sources are given below.

REFERENCING

52.   The Author-Date system (Harvard System) of referencing is recommended. It is accepted and understood by academic institutions and libraries throughout the world. It is used for literature and other media but equally it can be used for unpublished material and sources such as the internal documents of organizations and oral statements by individuals. Other methods such as footnotes and numbers in the text can be used but they increase the difficulty of typing a report and need constant page turning in reading. The Author-Date system is simpler for the student and it ties in well with recording of notes during the investigation.

53.   References in the text use the author`s name followed by the date the material was published, either in the form `Drucker 1967 says........`, or ` a number of authorities (Burns & Stalker 1961, Davenport 1950, Herzberg 1968) indicate that........`

54.   Where there are two co-authors both names are given, where there are more than two the name of the first and `et al` are used, eg, `Goldthorpe et al 1968`. If the material is the product of an organization, without a named author, the organization`s name can be used, eg, `National Health Service 1970`.  If it is necessary to refer to more than one publication by the same author in the same year the letters `a`, `b`, etc, are added to the date, eg, `DHSS 1993a`, `DHSS 1993b`.  The reference can be extended to locating the material by adding the page number after the date, eg, `Drucker 1967:135`   Unpublished documents such as other reports or teaching handouts can be referenced in the same way.  Oral statements can be shown too, eg, `Smith 1975`.

55.   The Reference section of the report lists all references in alphabetical order of authors' surnames. To trace the material accurately through the library system the reference contains the following elements in sequence:

a.   The author's name in block capitals followed by the initials. (eg, DRUCKER P F).

b.   The date of the publication, shown at the front of published material with the copyright sign. (eg, 1967).

c.   The title of the work, with only the first letter and any proper nouns in capitals, typed in bold or italic. If it is contained in a journal or larger publication the title of that is in bold or italic and the title of the work is left plain. (see Sadler 1974 below).

d.   The place of publication. (eg, London).

e.   The name of the publisher. (eg, Heinemann).

f.   For articles in journals the volume and issue number are given, with the pager numbers, after the publisher's name. (see Sadler 1974 below).

56.   The International Standard Book Number (ISBN) is unique to every edition of every published work and can be added to be precise but it is not normally used in reports unless the author has a specific reason to do so. The ISBN of this book is shown on the title page: ISBN 1 871053 05 6. The first number indicates the country, the next group of numbers the publisher, the next the actual edition, and the final number is a computer check number to establish the accuracy of the number. In the UK a list of all UK books in print is produced by Whitaker who are responsible for the issue of ISBN numbers. It is up-dated each month and is supplied to libraries on microfiche and to booksellers in a periodical. Some libraries also hold the the lists of USA books in print. Students can trace a book by author or title through the lists if they wish to borrow or purchase the book.

57.   For references needing more than one line, the extra lines are indented to give prominence to the author's name. The lines are single spaced with a blank space between entries. Examples:

BURNS T & G M STALKER 1961 Enterprise for everyman. in Lupton T (ed) 1970 *Payment systems*
        Harmondsworth: Penguin 181-199.

DHSS 1973a *HRC(73)3 Management arrangements for the re-organised NHS* London: Department of Health and
        Social Services.

DHSS 1973b *HRC(73)7 Operation and develoment of services: organisation for personnel
        management* London: Department of Health and Social Services.

DONOVAN LORD 1968 *Royal commission on trade unions and employers' associations report* London: HMSO.

DRUCKER P F 1967 *The effective executive* London: Heinemann.

GOLDTHORPE J H, D LOCKWOOD, F BECHHOFER & J PLATT 1968 *The affluent worker: industrial attitudes
        and behaviour* Cambridge University Press.

GOWER E 1987 *Complete plain words* Reference Books Harmondsworth: Penguin.

HERZBERG F 1868 One more time: how do you motivate employees? *Harvard Business Review*
        Vol 46 1968 53-62.

NATIONAL HEALTH SERVICE 1970 *Guide to good practice in hospital administration: Management Services
        (NHS) No1* London: HMSO.

ROGET P 1990 *Thesaurus of English words and phrases.* revised E M Kirkpatrick. Reference Books.
        Harmondsworth: Penguin.

SADLER P J 1974 Personnel policy in a changing society *Personnel Management* Vol 6 No 5 May 1974 26-29.

SMITH D E 1975 Research and Development Manager, Somesuch Limited, in an unrecorded conversation with
        the author in March 1975.

TABLES

58.   Tables are a useful way of presenting data. They should be kept as simple as possible: if they need to be complex they should be assigned to the appendices.   If they are placed in the text they are numbered `Table 1`, `Table 2`, etc, as they arise.   They should be placed as near as possible after the text they support, in a vertical (portrait) format, using the same margins as the text. Each table has its own heading, in bold lower case like a paragraph heading, and is placed at the foot of the table.   The headings should be single spaced but the data should be spaced in the same way as the text. Notes are added using bracketted numbers and the source should be shown if it is not originated by the author.   For example:

	No of Stoppages per 100,000 Employees (1)	No of Working Days lost per 1,000 Employees (1)
Australia	63.8	400
New Zealand	26.8	150
Canada (2)	15.8	970
United Kingdom	16.8	190

Notes: 1. In manufacturing and mining industries.

2. Excludes lockouts.

Source: Donovan 1968

Table 1.   Comparative International Strike Statistics 1964-68.

FIGURES

59.   Figures include diagrams, graphs, histograms, pie-charts, sketches and maps.   They may also include illustrations and photographs, although these may be designated separately as `Illustration 1`, `Illustration 2`, etc. If too complex they can be assigned to the appendices but if they are placed in the text they are numbered `Figure 1`, `Figure 2`, etc, as they arise. They should be placed as near as possible after the text they support. Each has its own heading, like a paragraph heading, and the wording is single spaced.   They should be kept as simple as possible and any symbols should be explained. They should be in the vertical (portrait) format, using the same margins as the text. If they are too large or too small photocopying can be used to bring them to the appropriate size.   Sources should be shown if they are not original. For example:

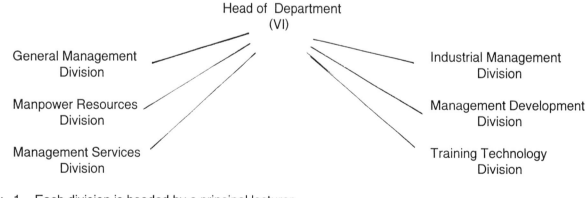

Notes: 1. Each division is headed by a principal lecturer.

2. There are eight departments in the College organization.

(VI) = Burnham Scale Head of Department Grade 6.

Figure 1.   Department of Management Some College of Technology Organization in 1974.

This example report uses the principles and conventions dealt with in Parts 1 to 5. It does not represent a particular standard in terms of academic qualifications, but it has been written to illustrate all those principles and conventions.

It is an example of a report that aims to satisfy the assessors for an academic qualification and at the same time to be of use to the management of the host organization that raised the issue and provided facilities for the investigation.

The report occupies 25 pages and contains about 6,000 words of original text. It deliberately includes most of the 'optional extra' parts of the report format to demonstrate their use, although it is a relatively short report.

Like Part 5 this report has been produced on personal computer using a word processing programme and a printer and therefore uses bold type face headings (see Part 5, para 39). Original material was first reduced by photocopying and then glued on to the A4 sheet before reproduction.

Note the hierarchy of headings used in a report of this size, and above. Note also that it is typed in one-and-a-half spacing on one side only of the A4 paper, with the left-hand margin 40mm and with the right-hand, top and bottom margins at least 15mm.

For the purpose of example, annotations have been made in the left-hand margin in the text of the report to show how it incorporates the structure of the investigatory process, as explained in Parts 1 to 5, eg:

Background

Issue
(=Problem)

Aim of Investigation

Method

Concepts

Evidence

Evaluation

Implications

What the
overall
situation is.

What could
happen
as a result.

What could
be done
about it.

What should
be done.

Such annotations would not be made in a real report..

LABOUR TURNOVER AND TRAINING OF SALES ASSISTANTS

AT ALL-INS RETAIL STORE

Submitted for the

Postgraduate Diploma in Management Studies

Norsex University

December 1993

ACKNOWLEDGEMENTS

The author wishes to acknowledge his indebtedness to all those who assisted and advised him during the project and especially:

Mrs Jill Smith, Staff Manageress, All-Ins Limited.

Miss Joan Brown, Staff Manageress, Ease Stores Limited.

The sales supervisors and sales assistants of All-Ins Limited.

Mr S Wilson, his Supervisor and Senior Lecturer in Management, Norsex University.

ABSTRACT

The issue was first stated as a problem in training replacement full-time sales assistants in a medium sized independent retail store in a large shopping centre. It involved 30 staff posts.

The investigation included discussion with the Staff Manageress, some supervisors and some assistants. Comparable details of staff numbers, pay and conditions, training and labour turnover rate were obtained from five similar stores in the same shopping centre. A job satisfaction questionnaire was applied to the assistants and to the assistants of one of the five other stores.

An underlying and more serious problem of high labour turnover coupled with low job satisfaction emerged soon in the investigation. Models of labour turnover analysis, job satisfaction, pay and conditions, and training were applied in the study.

Conclusions indicated an unhappy and disturbed workforce with the probability of a worsening condition, leading to a reputation as a bad employer, difficult customer relations, and serious commercial disadvantage.

Recommendations included expert job analysis for job redesign, person specifications and training design; improved pay and a modified working week; supervisor specification and training; and review of staff inter-relationships.

CONTENTS

CHAPTER 1   INTRODUCTION

'All-Ins' is a large retail store in a major shopping centre. Its stock is mainly ready-to-wear clothing, foods, travel goods, small electrical appliances and kitchen ware.   In this it is in competition with a number of similar stores in the centre. Unlike those, which are branches of multiple chains, 'All-Ins' is privately owned and has no other branches.

At the customer service level there are 30 full-time sales assistant posts and 30 part-time posts. The sales assistants are employed mainly on keeping the counter and display stands fully stocked, manning the cash tills and answering customer enquiries. They are entirely female and they work a 40 hour five-day week, on a roster from Monday to Saturday.   New staff are trained on the job. There are four supervisors for the sales staff, also on a rostered week.

Mrs Jill Smith, the Staff Manageress, stated that she had a major problem in training new full-time sales assistants to the right standards. So many came in each month that the supervisors and experienced staff could not give them the right attention. No new posts had been created in the past two years: the new staff were all replacements for ones who had left. Part-timers were no problem as they were given very limited responsibilities unless they had already had full-time experience of the work. Mrs Smith asked for help to resolve the problem.

The aim of the investigation was to identify factors in the training of replacement full-time sales assistants and to recommend remedies.

CHAPTER 2 METHOD

The main investigation was conducted full-time over a six week period in July and August 1993, with excellent co-operation from the Staff Manageress of All-Ins.

A number of detailed discussions were held with the Staff Manageress and these were augmented by informal discussions with sales staff supervisors and full-time sales assistants.

Limited information was obtained from the personnel staff of five similar local stores on pay, working conditions, staff numbers, training policy and labour turnover rates.

Detailed interviews or questionnaires covering all sales staff were not allowed because of sensitive staff relations, but a job satisfaction questionnaire was constructed. It was tried out first with a separate group of shop assistants as a pilot study. It was then was given to all full-time sales assistants, with a 93% response. The questionnaire was also given to the full-time sales assistants of a similar local store, with a 90% response. The questionnaire and its scoring method are shown in Appendix A.

CHAPTER 3   LABOUR TURNOVER

Although the problem posed was about training sales assistants, the training is needed for replacements. It was therefore decided first to look at the incidence and nature of labour turnover, among full-time assistants, which gives rise to replacements. Although there are a number of means of analysing labour turnover (ACAS 1981) the information available at All-ins limited the survey to labour turnover rate, cohort survival and some costs. As reasons for leaving, unfortunately, were not recorded a survey of job satisfaction was conducted.

LABOUR TURNOVER RATE

Concepts

Labour turnover rate (LTR) is conventionally the number of leavers in a period as a percentage of the number employed in the period:

$$LTR = \frac{\text{Number of leavers in period (eg, a year)}}{\text{Average Number employed in period}} \times 100 = \text{per cent}$$

It is used to show the magnitude of wastage, provided that the rate can be compared with the rate for similar employees in the same labour market, or with employees in the same jobs in previous periods.

Evidence

Fortunately, it was possible to obtain comparative information about five similar stores in the same shopping centre, all of them branches of multiple store chains. The turnover rate per year for All-Ins was 80%.   For the other five stores it was: Store B 15%,   Store C 24%, Store D 20%, Store E 10% and Store F 30%.

Implications

This indicated that All-Ins had a very serious problem of labour turnover, comparing very badly with the similar employers of similar labour in the shopping centre.

SURVIVAL

Concepts

The next consideration was the length of time new employees stayed with the store.   This is based on a well-founded theory first proposed by the Tavistock Institute of Human Relations (Rice et al 1950) which analyses the reaction of new employees in three phases:

    a.   **Period of Induction Crisis**. In the initial phase the new recruit is uncertain about relationships with co-workers and supervisors, ability to cope with the job, and the nature of the work. The recruit is emotionally sensitive and a minor setback in relationships or success may cause the recruit to leave. Care is needed in selection, supervision, training and work group placing to avoid crisis in this period of induction.

b.   **Period of Differential Transit.** Once the new employee has come to terms with the job and the work environment, he or she will begin to consider in a rational way the extent to which the work and conditions fit in with personal expectations of a job. The employee may then decide to leave. To avoid losses in this period of differential transit, care must be taken in selection, in not over-selling the job in the recruitment stage, and in reviewing pay and conditions in relation to the local labour market.

c.   **Period of Settled Connection.** In the third phase the employee identifies his or her future with the company and settles down to be a long-term employee.

Evidence

Analysis of the wastage out of a cohort of recruits can identify if there are any problems in the first two of these phases. Records of employees' starting and leaving dates were available. As this study was conducted in the Summer of 1993, it was decided to take as a cohort those full-time assistants who entered All-Ins in the 12 month period January to December 1992, thus allowing at least 6 months for wasting out. Analysis was not carried beyond the first 6 months of service accordingly.   Figure 1 shows the Survival Curve and the number leaving in each month of service.

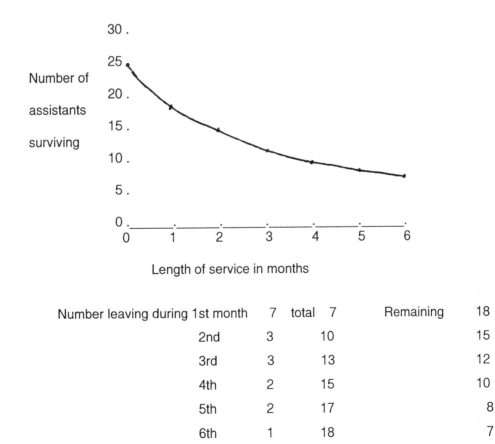

Number leaving during 1st month	7	total	7	Remaining	18
2nd	3		10		15
3rd	3		13		12
4th	2		15		10
5th	2		17		8
6th	1		18		7

Figure 1. Survival of 25 Full-time Sales Assistants entering All-Ins in the Year January to December 1992

9

It is quite clear from the curve and the figures that All-Ins has severe induction crisis among its new recruits: 28% leave in their first month. There are also severe losses in the 2nd and 3rd months to bring the loss to over a half of all recruits: this suggests that the expectations of a number of those surviving the induction period are not met in the differential transit period. A whole range of possible faults in selection, training, supervision, pay and conditions and work group arrangements is indicated.

Implications

JOB SATISFACTION

The reasons for full-time assistants leaving were not recorded, and with this type of employee accurate identification of a reason for every leaver is not easy to achieve. The propensity for individuals to leave a job has long been seen as resulting from two main factors: the level of job satisfaction and the visibility of an acceptable or better alternative (March & Simon 1958). For the latter the assistants are well aware of the opportunities in the same shopping centre for alternative jobs and the Staff Manageress stated that she often recognised past employees working in other stores and shops.

Concepts

Job satisfaction is the extent to which the employee's expectations for rewards and conditions are met. Low job satisfaction results in many problems: increased absenteeism, faulty work and leaving. Various methods are available to assess job satisfaction, often by interviews and discussions with staff. The Staff Manageress did not wish all staff to be interviewed in case it increased tensions. However, it was agreed to use a simple questionnaire survey.

The measure chosen was a job satisfaction survey which was influenced by the 'Job Description Index' (JDI) developed inthe USA by Smith et al (1969). This group conducted a very extensive survey of employees and concluded that job satisfaction had five main aspects: the intrinsic aspects of the work itself, pay, promotion prospects, supervision and relations with co-workers. They also concluded that these aspects were independent and that an individual could have different levels of satisfaction in each. They devised a simple questionnaire to measure the levels in each. Each aspect was represented by a section of questions or statements to which the the subject answers 'Yes' if it applies in his or her job, or 'No' if it does not apply, or '?' if not sure. Scoring in each aspect was on a scale from 0 (low) to 54 (high).

A similar questionnaire was constructed for the survey of All-ins' full-time sales assistants. The five aspects chosen were: work itself, pay, supervision, job prospects and fellow workers. Ten words or phrases appropriate to the UK work culture were used for each aspect. The responses were scored on a scale from 0 (low) to 30 (high) with 3 points given for a response that showed satisfaction, 0 points for one that showed dissatisfaction, and 1 point for an `undecided` response. After a pilot survey the questionnaire shown in Appendix A was used.

Method

10

While the scores can be seen as giving a good indication of levels of satisfaction, satisfaction itself depends on the individual's needs and expectations. The scores are therefore only relevant when they can be compared with other similar employees in similar jobs in the same local labour market. Fortunately the Staff Manageress of Store E, which has a very low labour turnover rate, was willing to apply the questionnaire to her 40 full-time sales assistants. In the event, with the incidence of sickness, absenteeism and vacancies, 28 assistants of All-Ins and 36 assistants of Store E completed questionnaires. As this represented a return of 93% and 90% respectively of the maximum possible survey, it was considered a useful insight into the levels of job satisfaction.

Evidence

The spread of scores from the two groups is shown in Figure 2. below.

Score	WORK ITSELF	PAY	SUPERVISION	JOB PROSPECTS	FELLOW WORKERS	Score
30						30
29	E		E			29
28			E			28
27	E		E		E	27
26	E		EEE		E	26
25	EEE		EEE		EE	25
24			EE		EE	24
23	EEE	E	EE	A E	EE	23
22	EE	E	EEE	E	EE	22
21	E	E	EE	E	EE	21
20	EEE	E	EEEEE	A	EEEE	20
19	EEEE	EE	EEE	A	EEE	19
18	A EEE	EE	EE	A E	EEE	18
17	A EEE	EE	EEE	A E	EEEE	17
16	A EE	A EEE	E	AAA EEE	A EE	16
15	A EEEE	AA EE	EE	AA EEEE	AAA E	15
14		EE	AA	AAAA EEE	A EEEE	14
13	A E	A	E		AA	13
12	A E	AA EEE	AA	AAA EEEEE	AA EE	12
11	AAAA E	AA EE		AAAAA EEE	A E	11
10	AAA	AAA EEEE	AAA	A EEEE	AAA	10
9	AAA E	AA E	AAA	AA E	A	9
8	AA	A EE	AA	A EE	AA	8
7	AAA E	AAA EE	AAAA	A EEE	AAA	7
6	A	AA E	A	A E	A	6
5	AAA	AAAAA E	AAA	E	AAA	5
4	A	A E	AA	E	A	4
3	A	A EE	AA		A	3
2		A	AA		A	2
1	A	A	AA		A	1
0					A	0

A = All-ins Assistants   (28 responses from a total of 30 = 93%)

E = Store E Assistants   (36 responses from a total of 40 = 90%)

Figure 2. Job Satisfaction Scores of Sales Assistants in All-Ins and Store E.

The results have the following implications:

a.   In Work Itself, All-Ins scores very low in relation to Store E. This suggests deficiencies in training, job design and work arrangements.

b.   The distribution of scores in Pay are slightly better for Store E but generally both sets reflect the relatively low rates of pay available in the retail trade.

c.   Supervision shows All-Ins in a poor light compared with Store E. This is a clear problem area.

d.   Distribution of Job Prospects scores are similar and reasonable for this type of employment. The relatively higher scores for All-Ins in this aspect may reflect the better chances for promotion in a high turnover situation.

e.   Again there is a great contrast between the two stores in Fellow Workers, with All-Ins showing up badly. It indicates a lack of cohesion and co-operation among staff, and a great deal of tension and unhappiness.

COSTS

The costs of high turnover cannot be ignored. There are human costs in the stress on supervisors and experienced employees who have to cope with additional work during vacancies and at the same time train newcomers. High turnover has a domino effect as it causes those remaining to think it might be wise to leave too, and so look round for other jobs. Not least it lowers the reputation of the employer: potential recruits may see the inability of the company to keep staff as a sign of a bad employer.

The financial costs could include damage and lost sales by new inexperienced staff, and these are not easy to measure. Any new starter incurs costs in advertising, application processing, testing, interviewing and documentation.   The Staff Manageress calculated this as an average of £350 for each starter. If it is assumed that a new assistant takes at least 4 weeks to reach a proficient level, it could be assumed that only about half of her labour cost (£120 per week wages + 30% overheads for national insurance, pensions, administration, etc = £156 per week) goes into productive work and the other half goes into learning the job. This represents a learning cost of £312 over the four weeks. Added to the recruitment cost of £350 this would suggest that it costs All-Ins £662 for each new starter. If the annual labour turnover rate were reduced from 80% to 20%, there would be a reduction from 24 to 6 new starters, saving 18 x £662 per year per starter = £11,916 per year.

In all, the survey shows up the major triggers that may cause assistants to quit from All-Ins: poor training, job design and work arrangements, low pay, inadequate supervisory skills, and low workgroup cohesion. It also shows the high financial and morale costs incurred.

CHAPTER 4 PAY AND CONDITIONS

Concepts

Job satisfaction is seen to be affected a great deal by pay and conditions. The perception of better alternative jobs arises from unfavourable comparisons with the pay and conditions enjoyed by sales assistants in other stores in the shopping centre. A comparison was therefore made with five other similar stores, in the proportion of full-time to part-time assistants, weekly pay, hours per week, and the working week in number of days and their distribution over the shopping week. The comparison is set out in Table 1, which also includes the training policy and the annual labour turnover rates.

Evidence

Store	Number of Assistants FT	Number of Assistants PT	Full-time Assistants: Weekly Pay	Weekly Hours	Days Worked	Training % Off Job	Training % On Job	Annual Labour Turnover Rate
All-Ins	30	30	£120	40	5 Mon-Sat	0	100	80%
B	40	60	£132	40	5 Mon-Sat	50	50	15%
C	42	22	£120	38	5 Mon-Sat	80	20	24%
D	55	60	£120	39	5 Mon-Fri	100	0	20%
E	40	10	£126	38	5 Tue-Sat	50	50	10%
F	20	30	£124	40	5 Mon-Sat	0	100	30%

Table 1. Comparison of Working Conditions, Training and Labour Turnover: All-Ins and Five Similar Local Stores

One significant factor in relation to turnover is the arrangement of the working week. Stores D and E have a continous 5 day week, with two consecutive days off, Store D because it mans its store with part-timer assistants only on Saturday, and Store E because it closes on Mondays. For the others, staff may have a broken week.

Another significant factor is pay. Although Store B has a spread 5 day week it has a low turnover rate, but it pays over £6 per week more than any other. The weekly hours of work may have some influence, but the differences are too small to show any significant effects.

The proportion of part-timers to full-timers does not appear to have any significance, except where part-timers are used by Store D to avoid Saturday working by the full-timers. The training policy may have some effects but that will be considered in the next chapter.

14

Implications

All-Ins compares badly with the other stores in pay and conditions: it has the lowest pay with the longest hours and requires its full-time assistants to work a rostered 5 day week over 6 days. Store D with the lowest turnover contrasts well with the highest pay but one, the lowest weekly hours, and a continuous 5 day Tuesday to Saturday week. It would be natural for All-Ins assistants to be attracted to jobs in other stores.

15

CHAPTER 5   TRAINING

Evidence

The original problem posed was the difficulty of providing adequate training for new sales assistants.   Enquiry into the training objectives and methods showed that it consisted of 'showing new staff how to do the job' and it was conducted entirely on the shop floor by supervisors and experienced staff. New recruits were expected to be working while learning. At busy times and when there were staff vacancies newcomers would receive little attention and would be expected to use their initiative.

There was no prescribed training programme to be followed by recruits.   In the past, in the store's more stable times, the system had worked with long-serving experienced supervisors and a low turnover of assistants. The introduction of new technology affecting sales staff had been limited to modern cash registers connected to computerised stock control, but this had been introduced satisfactorily by the manufacturer's representives demonstrating their use to supervisors and assistants in a special training programme.

SYSTEMATIC TRAINING

Concepts

As turnover had increased the flow of new recuits and as the older experienced supervisors had also left, it was apparent that a more structured approach was needed for the training of sales assistants. The model chosen to explore this was the 'Systematic Approach to Training' (Adamson 1985).   This approach prescribes the starting point of designing a training process as a detailed analysis of the job, to identify the components of knowledge, skill, attitudes and activities required by an efficient job holder.

The second stage is to define each of these components as a training objective, stated as terminal behaviour (with, if necessary, the standards to be reached, the conditions under which it will be performed, and its relative importance). It would be stated as 'At the end of the training the trainee will be able to do so-and-so (within such a standard, under such-and-such conditions)'. A test would then be designed for each objective, simulating real conditions as closely as practicable, to verify if the trainee had reached the objective.

The third stage is the review of potential trainees to establish which objectives they can already achieve and which they cannot, ie the 'gaps' to be bridged. The ability to 'do' certain objectives already might also be a required entry qualification. The tests established in the second stage would be used for this review.

The fourth stage is to provide an efficient and effective learning process, ie, one that will enable the trainees, by the cheapest methods, to reach all the 'gap' objectives fully.

16

The fifth stage is the evaluation of the training.   Effectiveness is assessed by following the trainee into the job to see to what extent he or she is able to perform all the components of the job to the standards defined and under the conditions in the job. Any discrepancies would then be fed back into the system to improve the training for later trainees. Efficiency is assessed by considering if the desired results could be achieved by any cheaper learning processes.

The system is illustrated in Figure 3 below.

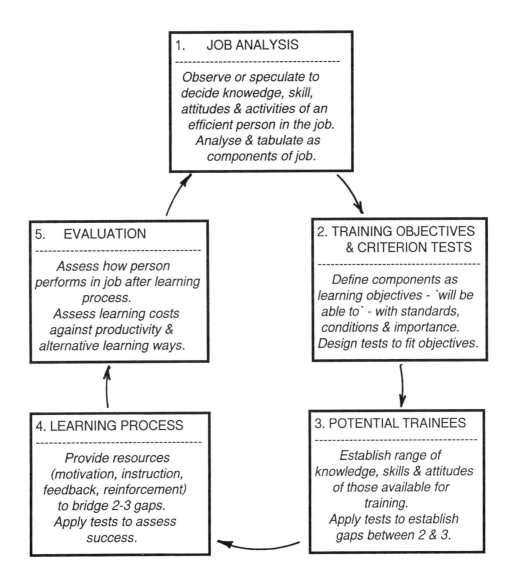

Source: Adamson (1985:15) Reproduced with permission.

Figure 3. The Systematic Approach to Training

17

TRAINING OBJECTIVES

Implications

The key to applying the system to training at All-Ins is the analysis of the job and the definition of the training objectives. The scope of this investigation did not permit a detailed analysis, and this would probably be better done by a trainer familiar with the retail trade. However, for guidance, some training objectives were proposed as examples and these are set out in Appendix B.

LEARNING PROCESS

Concepts

'On the job' training is not unusual in this type of employment, but it appears to have some disadvantages in the All-Ins context. It has been seen that there is serious induction crisis among new recruits and much of this may be due to the learning process. New trainees are affected by learning setbacks and where these occur in public, in the presence of other staff and customers, the emotional impact will be great. It was also seen from the job satisfaction scores that sales assistants rated supervision low and indicated a lot of dissatisfaction with co-workers. It is probable that the inability of supervisors to train and guide them effectively causes the former. The latter may arise partly because newcomers resent lack of help and criticism from more experienced staff, and experienced staff in turn resent the pressures they feel from carrying trainees.

The arguments for and against 'on the job' training are numerous: cheapness and reality against thoroughness and speed mainly. Off the job training requires special staff, accommodation and equipment, and requires minimum numbers of trainees to be economic. But it does provide a structured learning process without too many distractions and has its merits. A compromise is suggested by examination of the 'learning curve' phenomenom. Learning in a trainee to a specific standard of proficiency does not progress as a straight line over time. The learner progresses steadily for a while, then there is a period during which no progress is apparent. This plateau is then followed by a further steady rise, perhaps with other plateaus and steady rises until full proficiency is reached. It also appears that in terms of time, and therefore cost, the learner's progress slows down in the latter stage. One practical application of this phenomenom is a decision to end formal structured training at an optimum point and then allow the learner to complete the learning to the required full proficiency level by unstructured self-learning or on the job learning. The phenomenom and its application is dealt with in a number of texts, for example Kenney et al (1979). Figure 4 illustrates the learning curve.

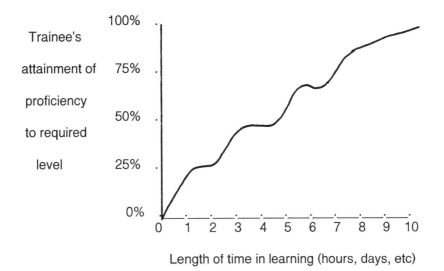

Figure 4. A Typical 'Learning Curve'

Stores B and E both have low labour turnover and Store E's assistants rated supervision and co-workers high in the job satisfaction analysis. Both conduct training 50% off the job and 50% on the job. It would seem sensible for All-ins to consider this practice too. The decision on the proportion of time off and on, and the sequence of the whole or parts of each, would be affected by the nature of the training objectives to be reached and the numbers and phasing of new recruits. Again this would need further study by a retail trade trainer.

19

CHAPTER 6   CONCLUSIONS

What the overall situation is

Although the training of replacement full-time sales assistants is a problem at All-Ins, it is aggravated by the even greater problem of high labour turnover.   Labour turnover is about four times more than the average among five similar stores in the same shopping centre.   There is serious induction crisis among new recruits, indicating faults in selection, training and supervision. Staff have considerable dissatisfaction with the work, pay, supervision and relations among co-workers.   Pay and conditions of work are inferior to those offered by competitors and the excessive labour turnover has high costs in staff morale and in money spent on recruiting and training replacements. Overall the picture is of an unhappy and unstable labour force.

What could happen as a result.

If this situation continues there is possibility of turnover increasing with a domino effect as the unsettled assistants remaining look around for other jobs. Poor relationships and attitudes among staff may also be perceived by customers, to the detriment of the store's 'goodwill'. The ultimate outcome could be a local labour market reputation as a 'bad company to work for' that would make it difficult to attract adequate numbers of good staff, and a customer reputation for poor service. Together these could lead to serious commercial difficulties in the highly competitive retail trade.

A number of possible courses of action could be followed to resolve the turnover and training problems. These are set out below.

What could be done about it.

SELECTION

At present it may be difficult for the store to be more selective with its current recruiting problems but it could aim to define more clearly the ideal characteristics of full-time sales assistants so that new recruits would be more likely to train successfully and stay with the company. This is considered further under 'Training' below.

TRAINING

A detailed analysis of the job could be made as the starting point for a number of actions. It would provide the basis for a well defined set of training objectives on which to establish a training system and the basis for a valid job description and person specification to be used in selection. An analysis at the same time could also provide a review of work arrangements and job design. It is possible that both of these two could be improved to give greater variety, interest and enrichment to the assistants' work and so provide greater satisfaction in that aspect.   The analysis is probably beyond the expertise and objectivity of the company's staff; it could require an external consultant with training and relevant retail trade expertise and therefore would have a cost. The benefits would make it worthwhile.

20

The possibility of a combination of off and on the job training could be explored. Again it would need expert advice, but that could be incorporated into the design of the complete training system with the job analysis above. The scale of recruiting may make it expensive to set up a separate training unit but there would be advantage in giving one of the four supervisors a specific training role, with some form of trainer training and some limited accommodation away from the shop floor. The costs would depend on the proportion of off the job training decided.

PAY AND CONDITIONS

Improved pay could reduce some losses of staff to competing stores. The ideal would be to raise it by £8 to match the majority. The annual cost would be 30 x 52 x £8 = £12,480, which is close to the suggested annual saving of £11,916 if turnover were reduced from 80% to the local average 20%. It must be admitted that improved pay alone would not reduce the turnover to that extent but there would be other savings in staff morale and ultimately customer relations.

Working conditions may be more cheaply improved. It is apparent from Stores D and E that there is an advantage in giving staff a continuous 5 day week. With 6 day opening this could be arranged by allocating some staff Monday to Friday and others Tuesday to Saturday. Saturday could be covered by increased use of part-timers and Monday is usually a slack shopping day needing less staff on duty.

SUPERVISION

With high turnover the selection and promotion of supervisors is severely constrained. They could be recruited from outside but there are advantages in morale and job knowledge in an internal promotion policy. The key again is the specification, job design and training. It might be possible to include this in the assistants' job analysis and training design. It is also possible to arrange for supervisors to attend the National Examinations Board for Supervisory Studies (NEBSS) certificate course at the local college. This would cost about £300 each for the year and on an afternoon and evening attendance basis would involve one afternoon away from work for a 35 week year. Alternative methods relevant to the specific roles of supervisors could be sought.

STAFF RELATIONS

Improvement of staff relations is likely to be gradual if some of the actions above were to be implemented. Directly, the tensions could be reduced by arranging social events such as staff outings. Other possible measures could be explored: more briefing of staff by senior management, greater participation in work arrangements, review of the grouping of staff at work, the use of group incentive payments. The limited scope of this study does not justify any more specific conclusions on these measures and further advice would be needed.

21

CHAPTER 7   RECOMMENDATIONS

The following recommendations are made:

What should be done.

1.   The company should employ a training consultant to analyse the sales assistants' job and to review job design, establish a training system and provide a job description and person specification for recruitment.

2.   Some initial off the job training should be considered on the basis of 1. above.

3.   The pay of full-time assistants should be increased by £8 per week.

4.   Full-time assistants should be allocated a 5 day continuous week: some Monday to Friday, others Tuesday to Saturday.

5.   The sales supervisors' job should be designed and specified clearly and they should be given relevant supervisory training.

6.   Methods to improve staff inter-relationships should be reviewed and advice should be sought.

JOB SATISFACTION QUESTIONNAIRE

Consider your present job and answer each of the five sections below.

WORK ITSELF

How well does each of these
words describe the work itself
in the job?

Tick: Yes ☐ if it does,
     No ☐ if it does not
     Undecided ☐ if you
     are not sure

Interesting	Yes ☐	No ☐	Undecided ☐
Boring	Yes ☐	No ☐	Undecided ☐
Useful	Yes ☐	No ☐	Undecided ☐
Satisfying	Yes ☐	No ☐	Undecided ☐
Respected	Yes ☐	No ☐	Undecided ☐
Dull	Yes ☐	No ☐	Undecided ☐
Tiresome	Yes ☐	No ☐	Undecided ☐
Good	Yes ☐	No ☐	Undecided ☐
Frustrating	Yes ☐	No ☐	Undecided ☐
Pleasant	Yes ☐	No ☐	Undecided ☐

PAY

How well does each of these
words or phrases describe the
pay you receive for your job?

Tick: Yes ☐ if it does
     No ☐ if it does not
     Undecided ☐ if you
     are not sure

Adequate	Yes ☐	No ☐	Undecided ☐
Bad	Yes ☐	No ☐	Undecided ☐
Excellent	Yes ☐	No ☐	Undecided ☐
Fair	Yes ☐	No ☐	Undecided ☐
Less than deserved	Yes ☐	No ☐	Undecided ☐
Underpaid	Yes ☐	No ☐	Undecided ☐
Exploited	Yes ☐	No ☐	Undecided ☐
More than enough	Yes ☐	No ☐	Undecided ☐
Well paid	Yes ☐	No ☐	Undecided ☐
Barely enough	Yes ☐	No ☐	Undecided ☐

SUPERVISION

How well does each of these
words or phrases describe the person
or persons who supervise you?

Tick: Yes ☐ if it does
     No ☐ if it does not
     Undecided ☐ if you
     are not sure

Praises good work	Yes ☐	No ☐	Undecided ☐
Inconsiderate	Yes ☐	No ☐	Undecided ☐
Knows job well	Yes ☐	No ☐	Undecided ☐
Easy to talk to	Yes ☐	No ☐	Undecided ☐
Rude	Yes ☐	No ☐	Undecided ☐
Inconsiderate	Yes ☐	No ☐	Undecided ☐
Listens to suggestions	Yes ☐	No ☐	Undecided ☐
Helpful	Yes ☐	No ☐	Undecided ☐
Leaves me to get on	Yes ☐	No ☐	Undecided ☐
Never there when needed	Yes ☐	No ☐	Undecided ☐

JOB PROSPECTS

How well does each of these
words or phrases describe your
chances of promotion in the job?

Tick: Yes ☐ if it does
     No ☐ if it does not
     Undecided ☐ if you are
     not sure

Good prospects for promotion	Yes ☐	No ☐	Undecided ☐
Good work is recognised	Yes ☐	No ☐	Undecided ☐
Dead end job	Yes ☐	No ☐	Undecided ☐
Fair promotion system	Yes ☐	No ☐	Undecided ☐
Few promotions from staff	Yes ☐	No ☐	Undecided ☐
Opportunities for training	Yes ☐	No ☐	Undecided ☐
Secure job	Yes ☐	No ☐	Undecided ☐
Reliable staff are promoted	Yes ☐	No ☐	Undecided ☐
No chance for promotion	Yes ☐	No ☐	Undecided ☐
Unfair promotions	Yes ☐	No ☐	Undecided ☐

FELLOW WORKERS

How well does each of these
words or phrases describe the people
you work with? (not customers)

Tick: Yes ☐ if it does
     No ☐ if it does not
     Undecided ☐ if you are
     not sure

Friendly	Yes ☐	No ☐	Undecided ☐
Lazy	Yes ☐	No ☐	Undecided ☐
Responsible	Yes ☐	No ☐	Undecided ☐
Cheerful	Yes ☐	No ☐	Undecided ☐
Good at the job	Yes ☐	No ☐	Undecided ☐
Unpleasant	Yes ☐	No ☐	Undecided ☐
Bright	Yes ☐	No ☐	Undecided ☐
Spiteful	Yes ☐	No ☐	Undecided ☐
Stupid	Yes ☐	No ☐	Undecided ☐
Helpful	Yes ☐	No ☐	Undecided ☐

Thank you.

23

JOB SATISFACTION QUESTIONNAIRE
SHOWING `SATISFIED` RESPONSES

If response agrees: score 3
" disagrees: score 0
" undecided: score 1

Consider your present job and answer each of the five sections below.

WORK ITSELF

How well does each of these
words describe the work itself
in the job?

Tick: Yes ☐ if it does,
No ☐ if it does not
Undecided ☐ if you
are not sure

Interesting	Yes ☑	No ☐	Undecided ☐
Boring	Yes ☐	No ☑	Undecided ☐
Useful	Yes ☑	No ☐	Undecided ☐
Satisfying	Yes ☑	No ☐	Undecided ☐
Respected	Yes ☑	No ☐	Undecided ☐
Dull	Yes ☐	No ☑	Undecided ☐
Tiresome	Yes ☐	No ☑	Undecided ☐
Good	Yes ☑	No ☐	Undecided ☐
Frustrating	Yes ☐	No ☑	Undecided ☐
Pleasant	Yes ☑	No ☐	Undecided ☐

PAY

How well does each of these
words or phrases describe the
pay you receive for your job?

Tick: Yes ☐ if it does
No ☐ if it does not
Undecided ☐ if you
are not sure

Adequate	Yes ☑	No ☐	Undecided ☐
Bad	Yes ☐	No ☑	Undecided ☐
Excellent	Yes ☑	No ☐	Undecided ☐
Fair	Yes ☑	No ☐	Undecided ☐
Less than deserved	Yes ☐	No ☑	Undecided ☐
Underpaid	Yes ☐	No ☑	Undecided ☐
Exploited	Yes ☐	No ☑	Undecided ☐
More than enough	Yes ☑	No ☐	Undecided ☐
Well paid	Yes ☑	No ☐	Undecided ☐
Barely enough	Yes ☐	No ☑	Undecided ☐

SUPERVISION

How well does each of these
words or phrases describe the person
or persons who supervise you?

Tick: Yes ☐ if it does
No ☐ if it does not
Undecided ☐ if you
are not sure

Praises good work	Yes ☑	No ☐	Undecided ☐
Inconsiderate	Yes ☐	No ☑	Undecided ☐
Knows job well	Yes ☑	No ☐	Undecided ☐
Easy to talk to	Yes ☑	No ☐	Undecided ☐
Rude	Yes ☐	No ☑	Undecided ☐
Inconsiderate	Yes ☐	No ☑	Undecided ☐
Listens to suggestions	Yes ☑	No ☐	Undecided ☐
Helpful	Yes ☑	No ☐	Undecided ☐
Leaves me to get on	Yes ☑	No ☐	Undecided ☐
Never there when needed	Yes ☐	No ☑	Undecided ☐

JOB PROSPECTS

How well does each of these
words or phrases describe your
chances of promotion in the job?

Tick: Yes ☐ if it does
No ☐ if it does not
Undecided ☐ if you are
not sure

Good prospects for promotion	Yes ☑	No ☐	Undecided ☐
Good work is recognised	Yes ☑	No ☐	Undecided ☐
Dead end job	Yes ☐	No ☑	Undecided ☐
Fair promotion system	Yes ☑	No ☐	Undecided ☐
Few promotions from staff	Yes ☐	No ☑	Undecided ☐
Opportunities for training	Yes ☑	No ☐	Undecided ☐
Secure job	Yes ☑	No ☐	Undecided ☐
Reliable staff are promoted	Yes ☑	No ☐	Undecided ☐
No chance for promotion	Yes ☐	No ☑	Undecided ☐
Unfair promotions	Yes ☐	No ☑	Undecided ☐

FELLOW WORKERS

How well does each of these
words or phrases describe the people
you work with? (not customers)

Tick: Yes ☐ if it does
No ☐ if it does not
Undecided ☐ if you are
not sure

Friendly	Yes ☑	No ☐	Undecided ☐
Lazy	Yes ☐	No ☑	Undecided ☐
Responsible	Yes ☑	No ☐	Undecided ☐
Cheerful	Yes ☑	No ☐	Undecided ☐
Good at the job	Yes ☑	No ☐	Undecided ☐
Unpleasant	Yes ☐	No ☑	Undecided ☐
Bright	Yes ☑	No ☐	Undecided ☐
Spiteful	Yes ☐	No ☑	Undecided ☐
Stupid	Yes ☐	No ☑	Undecided ☐
Helpful	Yes ☑	No ☐	Undecided ☐

Thank you.

24

EXAMPLES OF TRAINING OBJECTIVES FOR SALES ASSISTANTS AT ALL-INS

At the end of training the trainee should be able to:

Identify shortages of stock on the counters and display stands.

Transfer articles from the stockroom to the store and record the transaction.

Answer a customer's question about the location of products in the store.

Respond to a customer's complaint in a conciliatory manner.

Receive returned goods from a customer and provide the replacement or refund.

Operate the cash till.

Process a cash card transaction

Process a cheque and cheque card transaction.

Identify potential thieves.

Conduct the process of challenging a thief and calling in the supervisor.

The conditions under which all the objectives will be performed are within the confines of the store and during hours on duty.

The standards expected would be such that no damage is done to the store`s sales efficiency or to good customer relations.

All the objectives are seen to have equal importance.

25

REFERENCES

ADAMSON A 1985 *A systematic approach to training* Slough College.

ADVISORY, CONCILIATION & ARBITRATION SERVICE 1981 *Advisory booklet No 4: labour turnover* London: HMSO.

KENNEY J P J, E L DONNELLY & M A REID 1979 *Manpower training & development* London: Institute of Personnel Management.

MARCH J G & H A SIMON 1958 *Organizations* New York: Wiley.

RICE A K, J M HILL & E L TRIST 1950 The representation of labour turnover as a social process *Journal of Human Relations* No 3 1950.

SMITH P C, L M KENDALL & C L HULIN 1969 *The measurement of job satisfaction in work and retirement* Chicago: Rand McNally.